DUTCH ACADEMY FOOTBALL COACHING (U10-11)

Technical and Positional Practices from Top Dutch Coaches

HENK MARIMAN

HAN BERGER

LOUIS COOLEN

Published by

SOCCER TUTOR
.COM

DUTCH ACADEMY FOOTBALL COACHING (U10-11)

Technical and Positional Practices from Top Dutch Coaches

First Published August 2015 by SoccerTutor.com

Info@soccertutor.com | www.SoccerTutor.com

UK: 0208 1234 007 | **US:** (305) 767 4443 | **ROTW:** +44 208 1234 007

ISBN: 978-1-910491-05-8

Original Dutch Publishers

DeVoetbalTrainer ©, All Rights Reserved www.devoetbaltrainer.nl

Edited by

Alex Fitzgerald - SoccerTutor.com

Cover Design by

Alex Macrides, Think Out Of The Box Ltd.
Email: design@thinkootb.com Tel: +44 (0) 208 144 3550

Diagrams

Diagram designs by SoccerTutor.com. All the diagrams in this book have been created using SoccerTutor.com Tactics Manager Software available from www.SoccerTutor.com

Note: While every effort has been made to ensure the technical accuracy of the content of this book, neither the author nor publishers can accept any responsibility for any injury or loss sustained as a result of the use of this material.

Contents

Contents

Contents

Coach Profiles

Former Club Brugge Academy Director and AFC Ajax Assistant Academy Director

- UEFA A Licence and TVJO PRO (Professional Academy Director Course)
- 2011–2012: Club Brugge KV Technical Director
- 2007–2011: Club Brugge KV Academy Director
- 2004–2007: Germinal Beerschot Academy Director
- 1999–2004: Germinal Beerschot / Ajax Assistant Academy Director
- Coached Mousa Dembele, Jan Verthongen and Thomas Vermaelen

Henk Mariman

Chairman of the Dutch Professional Coaches (CBV)

- UEFA Pro Licence
- 2009-2015: Australia National Team Technical Director
- 2005-2008: De Graafschap Technical Director
- 2000-2003: FC Utrecht Technical Director
- 1998–2000: Netherlands U21 Head Coach
- 1993–1995: Sparta Rotterdam Head Coach
- 1983–1986: FC Groningen Head Coach
- 1976–1983 and 1987–1989: FC Utrecht Head Coach

Han Berger

Former Zenit St. Petersburg Academy Director

- UEFA Pro Licence
- 2011–2015: Zenit St. Petersburg Academy Director
- 2005–2007: FC Eindhoven Head Coach
- 2001–2005: Roda JC Assistant Coach
- 1996–2001: Helmond Sport Head Coach
- 1993–1996: UDI '19 Head Coach
- 1987–1993: Helmond Sport Assistant Coach
- 1985–1987: Helmondia '55 Head Coach
- 1982–1985: RKSV Nuenen Head Coach

Louis Coolen

CHAPTER 1

BASIC PRINCIPLES

Learning Basic Tasks and Positioning

- Consciously learn to play together
- 7v7 Small Sided Games
  (or 9v9 using 1-3-2-3 formation)
- Determining talent for certain positions
- Limited tactical instructions

General Description

- Develop understanding and sense of team play
- Develop understanding of individual roles in relation to a team game
- Develop understanding of actions without the ball (movement to receive or movements away from the ball)
- Within small sided games, it is necessary to teach basic functions that are associated with specific positions to determine the preference and talent for each player
- Perfect ability to develop technique

Guidelines

- Functional competitive actions with the ball including receiving with a good first touch, dribbling, passing, 1v1 duels, etc.
- Competitive actions with loss of possession: 1v1 duel games
- Competitive game play: 1v1 to 4v4 duels
- Competitive small sided games with variations, focusing on maintaining possession
- Changeovers - learn the basics in game situations
- Dynamic stretching in the warm up
- Number of training sessions per week: 3 (+1 match)
- Maximum duration of training = 75 minutes

CHAPTER 2

AGE SPECIFIC CHARACTERISTICS

Age Specific Characteristics (U10 - 11)

- The 'Golden Age'
- The first outline of the team awareness is visible

Here we are in the midst of the 'golden age' where players learn a lot very quickly and not only technically. The mental aspect provides an extra incentive, as they want to compete with the others and will therefore be driven to work. They want to be the best! This allows for a different mental approach to their own performance and that of others, as they become very critical. As a coach, it is our job to lead this process in the right direction using individual feedback, individual work items and evolution to self-evaluation which helps the players to develop themselves. It is all about the development and training and not the match result. When training young players, you must take the initial situation into account. Increasingly involve controlling the ball in all situations, from an end in itself to achieving the ultimate goal of developing the team awareness.

Players become more involved with each other. They see differences between teammates, who can do certain aspects better, and who (so far) is struggling. You need to be aware if the practice has 'worked'.

Children of this age generally have the same concentration levels. Targeting in the game and also in the exercise develops. Teamwork will get more meaning, and that manifests itself in developing the decision making component and a greater understanding of the opposition.

Within the game (7v7) there is understanding and caring for dealing with space. You will notice when training this age group that the players no longer just huddle together round the ball. There is more of an attempt for proportional distribution across the space (half-court) to achieve 'teamwork', where all the players take a certain role and contribute to the team effort. However, a balanced team organisation is still far from complete. Even within 7v7, the ball is often still a magnet to some extent. The players are still attracted to the ball and still have no clear picture as to when to move away from the ball.

CHAPTER 3

TRAINING / COACHING

Training / Coaching

Training is used to simplify the competition. Development features like the big game drive, the willingness to work and the will to win of the Under 11 age group should be translated to be educational and about coaching to goals. Concretely, this means that the players should be helped to learn to play together in a 7v7 situation by the coach, to develop their individual technique and to recognise the general principles to attack and defend. This all aids their development of insight into the game.

Training is to simplify the game. We play 7v7 on half a pitch. To make it clearer and simpler for the players, the number of players in the practices/ sessions is reduced. Due to the simplification of the resistance and the grouping of the objectives of the initial situation, the training content is determined. This results in 3 +GK, 2 +GK or 2v1 duels. In these situations the coach should always check all things are correct, such as the direction of play, player positions, performance, speed and the time of play.

Coaches should organise training so players are forced to make decisions. Based on what he sees, the coach coaches. He uses game insight to influence movement, actions and the individual decision making of the players. He observes the communication between the players, because the actions of the individual football players needs to be matched/connected to others. Paint a picture for the players and talk well with this age group as they will absorb the information.

The collective game up close from 4v4/5v5 practices is expanded into a 7v7 or 8v8 learning environment using half a pitch. The short game evolves into a larger playing area. The players progress from making 10-15 yard passes to making 15-20 yard passes.

During the warm-ups for competitive games we can also work on technical aspects. Up to and including the under 13 players, during the warm-up we practice with the ball and work on all sorts of movements within a small space for about ten minutes. When the players play in competitive games they can start to see that 'the boss is on the ball'. That does not necessarily happen in a positional game. A player must have the leadership and the coach checks the implementation.

CHAPTER 4

MATCHES

Matches

- 8v8 (3-2-3 formation) or 9v9 (4-2-3 formation)
- Talks and discussions almost always include questions, but should not be too long

The Coach's Role

The fun and enjoyment of training is of paramount importance. Players need their space to freely produce good football. The emphasis is on the art and the basics of tactics start to be created. For example, we focus on possession and movement into space to receive. Coaching points always include questions but should not take up too much time. We give a limited number of instructions to the team e.g. two main points to focus on when in possession and two for when the opposition have possession. The coach will be clearly present during matches, but only indicates the broadly consistent themes of positioning and occupying space. With this, he helps the players. If the players position themselves relative to each other, they create more opportunities and options for their team mates.

It is not intended for the coach to choose the passes or determine the players' decision making. We provide space for them to use their own insight and creativity. Errors will be made, but the players will learn for the next time they are in a similar situation. For example, after a player shoots on goal when a team mate was in a better position, it is very easy and

tempting to shout instructions before the situation, but it is important for them to take their own decision at that time. The best thing to do is to ask the player afterwards if he chose the best solution. Mistakes will be made, but the focus should be on what the player intended to do. Of course you can sometimes find in this age group that there is already a good awareness of the game or that some players are influenced by the coach's instructions from training sessions and before the game. This is best achieved if the instructions are calm and not emotive, which works much less well. The intent is for players to absorb information and then use their experiences to learn and play better. At this age, you do not want to attach too many limitations or 'tactics' because it is mainly about the training of basic skills. Give players the space and time to use these skills in the game. A coach must also not be influenced by the environment or by disputes. He must know what matters and that is the development of his players. He is therefore not focused on the result in terms of winning and losing the match. Look through the eyes of the individual development of the player, with a balance between maximum fun and the greatest possible progression within the development process.

The Role of the Parents

The parents are present and play an important role. Fortunately, some parents follow their child's football development. Their enthusiasm is very important for the football experience of children. Many parents, however, do not encourage their children in the right way and the child can then often be an extension of the experience of their parent/s. Encouragement is important but parents should not coach from the sideline. Otherwise, before you realise, there are twice as many coaches along the line as there are players on the pitch.

In addition, for some parents, the outcome of the match and the position in the league table are more important than the pleasure and development of the children's football. From this thought the parents can interfere with the game in all sorts of ways. They can try to influence practice or the handling of the rules and thus the result of the match. Both coaches and parents have a big responsibility, as they are partly responsible for the enjoyment of the whole team and each player. For the coach, it is extremely important to make clear what role parents have while the matches are being played.

It is all about earning game experience for the children. Children develop most rapidly in a safe learning environment. It is extremely important that the players are able to develop in an atmosphere in which the children are allowed the freedom to explore the game itself.

The child is helped by a person, the coach. That structure should be very clear. If not, then it can be confusing and the children no longer understand where they are supposed to be and what they are supposed to do. Parents are certainly necessary and absolutely welcome along the line. In addition, assistance from parents for the coach is often indispensable. As long as the children feel free to express themselves without fear and have positive encouragement, then everything will work out for the best. Give the child the opportunity!

Building 8 v 8 And 9 v 9 Small Sided Games

For competitive matches with younger players we start with 5v5. For this age group, we play 8v8 and in training and then progress to 9v9 small sided games.

5v5 Small Sided Games

When playing 5v5 at younger ages you choose to play with a diamond formation (1-2-1) automatically.

8v8 Small Sided Games

Within an 8v8 game the formation resembles the diamond used in 5v5 games. In principle the formation selected for 8v8 is the 3-1-3. As a result, the transition from 5v5 to 8v8 for children is easier. Both formations give approximately the same structure. In addition, the same principles are used in an 8v8 game as in an 11v11 game. This is very important for when the players progress to play on a larger pitch.

9v9 Small Sided Games

We progress to play 9v9 in a 60 x 65 yard area. This works as a perfect transition to playing 11v11 on a full pitch. When playing 9v9 games we set up a 3-2-3 formation, so have three lines (defence, midfield and attack). This creates triangles throughout the pitch and there are defenders, midfielders, wide players and a striker. We play without offsides and with big goals.

Play the games with short corners for this age group, as it is not time yet to practice full set pieces. We still play with junior football rules as we notice that in this age group there is still a lot of ball losses, over and over again. There are many moments of transition and players do not have much time to get back into a good position, because by then their team has lost the ball again.

CHAPTER 5

TRAINING SESSIONS

Training Sessions

- It should be fun for the players

- Competitive practices/drills

- A limited number of practices/drills per session

- The sessions must be process-oriented and built up over a period of time

- The coach needs to be able to increase or decrease the level of the practices/drills easily

- The sessions must be adapted to the technical development for each age group

It Should Be Fun for the Players

The perception of the players is the foundation of each method. Good training sessions should excite the players.

Competitive Practices/Drills

Competitive practices/drills with real resistance from opponents, teammates and limited time and space are the basis of learning for young football players. However, there are isolated technical practices (technical ball control exercises, passing etc) which are also very important. Combine both together within a session. If we ensure that isolated technical training is adapted and taken into the competitive drills, the players can then accelerate their development.

A Limited Number of Practices/Drills Per Session

A youth coach should not choose too many different practices for their session at the expense of the training time. Young players need time to get used to each practice and sometimes you only see the true rewards at the end. It is therefore better to have regular repetitions. A training session can contain up to 3 or 4 practices. In addition, simple practices move more quickly and guarantee more ball touches for each player.

The Sessions Must Be Process-Oriented and Built Up Over Time

If we want to profoundly influence the development process, there should be a process-oriented structure. You need to systematically build up training sessions with substance over time to get the best results. To start each training session with new practices/drills will provide too little a return on the time invested. Each practice must be repeated several times to provide a development impact.

The coach needs to be able to increase or decrease the level of the practices/drills easily

The level of the practice should be easy to modify:

- Adapt the resistance level
- Increase or decrease the difficulty by changing the amount of space and time etc
- Adapt the organisation (limited).

Key Point:

The sessions must be adapted to the technical development for each age group

Dutch Academy Football Coaching (U10-11)

CHAPTER 6

TECHNICAL TRAINING

Technical Training

For the youngest children (5/6 year olds) the ball is the greatest resistance. We work on ball control and dribbling, so the boss is on the ball. We have playful practices with many variations. For the technical movements with the ball, we use only a small number of movements in this phase, such as dribbling/turning with the inside of the foot, the outside of the foot and with the sole of the foot.

To learn a movement like the scissors, start individually with the ball and practice quickly in an open space. Scissors must then be done through a small space (in between 2 cones). The cones act as 'the opponent' but they are stationary. The next step is for the coach (or teammate) to replace the cones and act as a passive defender, so the players learn to perform the move with some resistance and the coach can give individual instructions.

The coach should pay particular attention to whether or not the movement is performed at the correct time, the players use the correct speed of execution and that the players use their whole body to perform the move with conviction. The next step is to use an active defender to increase the difficulty. This replicates a true 1v1 situation. It is very important to work in steps so the players develop in the best way.

In addition to all the technical movements we pay attention to receiving the ball also. Technique is not only the scissors and other turns or moves to beat. There are a variety of different ways to receive the ball, such as receiving without pressure, receiving with an opponent in front of you, next to you, behind you, and so on. There are also several follow-up actions that are very important for the decision making process. In one situation the best solution may be to play a short pass, and at another time it can be to play a long pass, shoot at goal or try to beat an opponent in a 1v1 situation. Training the receiving of the ball integrates perfectly into the technical programme. Each training session ends with the application of these movements, e.g. in a 1v1 duel with finishing.

In the training practices/drills to follow in the oncoming chapters, the emphasis is on applying the skills and slowly increasing the resistance level.

Teaching Technical Movements

Teaching technical movements happens according to a certain road map. Depending on the level of the player that can be shorter or longer. Because children nowadays are visually highly sensitive (television, computers and games consoles) the 'picture' becomes very important.

How Movement Can be Demonstrated:

- The coach makes the movement to visually display an example
- The coach makes the movement very slowly and talks the players through it (step by step)
- The coach makes the movement very slowly and the players do so at the same time while listening to the explanation
- Players practice their technical movements and the coach walks around and checks
- As the players get used to the movement, the speed can be increased

Fundamental Technical Abilities

Dribbling

- Keep the ball close to the feet with soft touches
- Make sure you are able to quickly change direction when running with the ball
- Be aware of the defender and shield the ball (use the body as a barrier between the defender and the ball)
- Do not go too close to the defender
- Make sure a feint is done at the right time, otherwise the ball will be blocked
- Make sure you accelerate during and after any action, otherwise you are easy to defend against

Passing

- Look behind and around you before receiving the ball and then look ahead for passing options
- Look for opportunities to play in behind the opposition defence
- The correct weight of pass is key - do not play it too soft, too hard, too high etc
- Play simple and play with the inside of the foot
- Play the ball in front of a moving player to run onto
- Play the ball towards your teammate's stronger foot and away from the opposing player
- Play the pass along the ground whenever possible and make sure the ball isn't bouncing
- Use a variety of short and long passes

Receiving and Ball Control

- Cushion the ball (take the speed off the pass)
- Do not let the ball bounce too far away from you
- Take the ball at the correct angle (and receive with the back foot) so that after receiving the ball, you are facing the direction you want to play in and can move forwards

- After receiving well with an open body shape (and with the back foot), it should be easy to then perform the next action i.e. pass or dribble
- Use your body to shield the ball from your opponent when receiving a pass (use your body as a barrier in between the ball and the defender)

Shooting

- Move the ball away from the defender to create space and an angle to shoot
- Use your body to shield the defender from the ball
- Look at the position of the goalkeeper and where the goal is - try to place the ball into the corner (accuracy is the key)
- Use the inside or outside of the foot to shoot past the goalkeeper (short distance) or use the instep for longer distances

Heading

- While the ball is travelling, look at a position where you can aim the header on target
- Look at the goalkeeper's position and place it with the head past the goalkeeper

Throw-ins

- Throw the ball to your teammates's strongest foot
- Look at the position of the player you are throwing to
- The player receiving needs to move into space
- Throw the ball with the correct weight - do not throw it too soft, too hard, too high etc

CHAPTER 7

TECHNICAL PRACTICES: MOVES TO BEAT

Practice Format

Each practice includes clear diagrams with supporting training notes such as:

- Name of Practice
- Objective of Practice
- Description of Practice
- Variation or Progression (if applicable)
- Coaching Points

Key

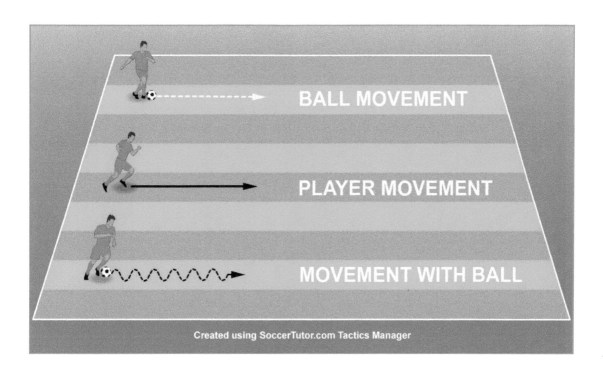

BALL MOVEMENT

PLAYER MOVEMENT

MOVEMENT WITH BALL

Created using SoccerTutor.com Tactics Manager

THE TECHNICAL BLOCK
8 Technical Practices in a Ball Control Exercise

1

Created using SoccerTutor.com Tactics Manager

2

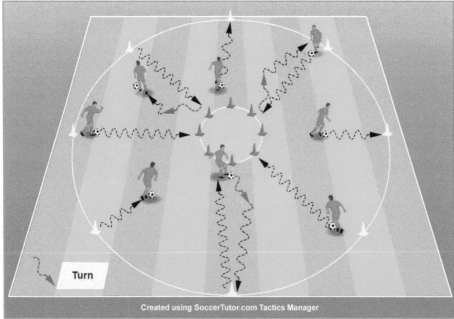

Turn

Created using SoccerTutor.com Tactics Manager

Objective

To practice technical movements to perfect ball control, turning and moves to beat.

Description

For this exercise we mark out a circle using 8 cones as shown in the diagram (diameter of 10-15 yards). We also mark out a smaller circle with 8 cones that has a diameter of 2-3 yards. A maximum of 16 players can take part.

In this circle exercise you can practice the following techniques which (except for receiving) are used to turn away from a defender (fully explained on the following pages):

Practice 1 - Receiving
Practice 2 - The Scissor
Practice 3 - 180° Chop
Practice 4 - The Chop Back Heel
Practice 5 - 90° Turn
Practice 6 - The Elastic Drag (or Flip Flap)
Practice 7 - The 'V' Move
Practice 8 - The Train (Stop and Go)
Practice 9 - Hip Feint and Change Direction

Diagram 1: The players simply practice the different technical movements in the free space outside the small circle, making sure to avoid collisions with their teammates. The movements should still be performed at speed and is if away from a defender.

Diagram 2: One player is positioned on each outside cone and they dribble the ball forwards towards the inside circle. When a player dribbles the ball from the outside cone to the inside cone, he then makes a 90° or 180° turn and dribbles back to the outside cone.

Progressions

1. Take away the inside cones and the coach stands in the middle instead. Each time a player approaches, the coach steps out to offer passive resistance for their turn.

2. Put the cones back to create the inside circle again. This time when one player is dribbling the ball and turning, another player jogs alongside him to provide passive resistance.

3. When one player is dribbling the ball and turning, we have a fully active defender next to him trying to win the ball. This creates a 1v1 duel with full resistance. The aim of the ball carrier is to dribble forwards, turn at the inside cone and then make it back to the outside cone.

PRACTICE 1: Receiving

Half the players in the exercise have a ball. The players dribble around the area and then pass the ball to a teammate who is free and in space. They practice receiving the ball in 3 different ways:

1. Receive with right foot -> 2. Receive with left foot -> 3. Receive on the move

PRACTICE 2: The Scissor

1. Dribble the ball with the head up.

2. Step over the ball diagonally with the right foot (the left foot moves across behind).

3. With the outside of the left foot, take the ball in the other direction and move away.

PRACTICE 3: **180° Chop**

1. Dribble the ball with the head up.

2. Right knee up with the leg angled behind the ball. The right toes strike the ball back and let the ball roll across the body.

3. Rotate your body as the ball rolls back. The outside of the left foot pushes the ball away to complete the turn.

PRACTICE 4: **The Chop Back Heel**

1. Dribble the ball with the head up.

2. Take a big step and plant your standing leg beyond the ball. Use the inside of the right foot to take the ball away at a 90° angle.

3. Turn around and make sure you immediately have control of the ball.

PRACTICE 5: **90° Turn**

1. Dribble with the ball close to the feet and with the head up.

2. Roll the ball back with the sole and move the right foot back to open up the body.

3. Use your arms to keep your balance, then touch the ball with the inside or outside of the right foot away.

PRACTICE 6: **The Elastic Drag (or Flip Flap)**

1. Dribble the ball with complete control using the right foot and with the head up.

2. Drag the ball with the inside of the right foot to the left and drop the left shoulder without losing contact with the ball.

3. Then quickly use the outside of the right foot (still retaining contact with the ball) to move the ball in the opposite direction (towards the right).

PRACTICE 7: The 'V' Move

1. Dribble the ball to one side, in this example to the left.

2. Place your right foot on the ball and roll it towards yourself with the sole of the right foot. Open up your body to the right hand side.

3. Take the ball with the inside (or outside) of the foot in the other direction (right) and accelerate away.

PRACTICE 8: The Train (Stop and Go)

1. Dribble forwards and keep the ball close using the outside of the foot.

2. Slow down and place the sole of your foot on the ball.

3. After slowing down or stopping, you then accelerate quickly forwards with the ball.

Dutch Academy Football Coaching (U10-11)

PRACTICE 9: Hip Feint and Change Direction

Created using SoccerTutor.com Tactics Manager

1. Turn your hip in, feint to kick the ball and then turn towards the left.

2. Change the body position towards the right and use the inside of the left foot to change direction.

3. Accelerate away with the ball.

SESSION 1: RECEIVING

SESSION 1: Receiving

Objective

To develop the basic technique of receiving the ball.

Description

Demonstrate a good example of the proper technique to receive with the inside of the foot, or let a technically skilled player demonstrate. Once the players understand how to receive with the inside of the foot, do the same for receiving the ball with the outside of the foot and the sole. In addition, practice taking a small touch and a bigger touch to push the ball further away.

Receiving the ball is one of the basic technical skills in football. The ball must do exactly what the player wants. The better the ball is controlled, the more time the player has to perform the next action. After receiving the ball, the player can choose to pass, to dribble, to turn or beat the nearest opponent. The choice for this is dependent on the specific situation.

Within youth football it is almost standard to use the inside of the foot when receiving the ball. At that time, it is also important to emphasise why the ball must often be received first:

"When you first take the ball with a good touch, it is then easier to play a pass. You can then focus better. Otherwise the ball can jump all over the place."

Older players, and particularly central players that are anticipating the ball along the ground, often choose to receive with the outside or sole of the foot. This allows the players to keep a distance between the ball and the opponent (behind them) to protect/shield the ball and retain possession.

    Dutch Academy Football Coaching (U10-11)

Passing and Receiving in Pairs in an Open Space

Objective

To develop the basic technique of receiving the ball within pairs.

Description

In an open space, each pair has a ball. The size of the area depends on the amount of pairs in the exercise. The players practice passing and receiving within the space. The coach can apply special rules and variations which are listed below.

Variations

1. Use a larger space with a higher ball speed.

2. Use a smaller space so the players have to use good awareness when receiving the ball. The players need to look up and avoid bumping into other players.

3. Add a compulsory movement before the pass arrives. The players can move towards the ball and then away to receive or move away and then move towards the ball to receive. (This variation is shown in the diagram)

4. After receiving the pass, the players must make a quick movement with the ball to the right or left.

Dutch Academy Football Coaching (U10-11)

Passing and Receiving in Pairs with Directional First Touch

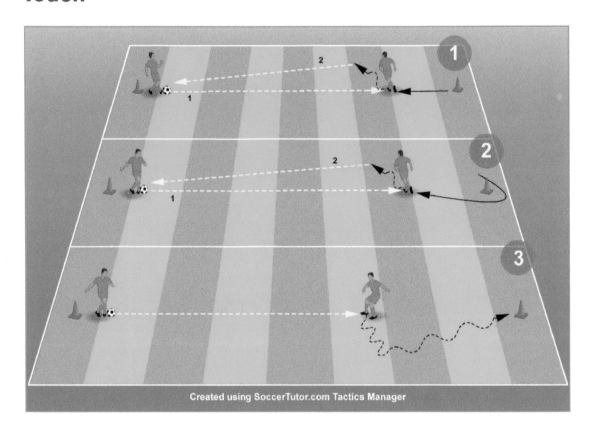

Created using SoccerTutor.com Tactics Manager

Objective

To develop the basic technique of receiving the ball and making a good directional first touch into space to prepare for the next action.

Description

The players work in pairs and are positioned on cones 15 yards apart. The first player passes the ball and the second player has to take a directional first touch and then perform a second action. The 3 different variations in the diagram are listed below.

Variations

1. The player moves forward to receive the pass, takes a directional first touch out in front towards the left or right and then passes the ball back to the other player.

2. This is the same as the first, but the player makes a movement around the cone before receiving, as shown in the diagram.

3. The player moves forward to receive the pass on the half turn, takes a directional first touch with the inside of the foot, turns in one movement and dribbles the ball to the cone.

Dutch Academy Football Coaching (U10-11)

Accurate Passing and Receiving in Between Cones

Description

In a 10 x 30 yard area, we have 2 players working together with a cone gate (1 yard) in between them. The dimensions can be adjusted for the age/level of the players. The first player passes through the cone gate and the second player takes a good directional first touch and passes back through the cone gate. The sequence continues and the players must always use 2 touches.

Coaching Points for Receiving with the Inside of the Foot

1. Before receiving the ball, the players should already know what they are going to do. This practice forces the players to be aware of where their teammate is (and this also helps to know where the opponents are later).

2. Make sure to be in the correct position before the first touch, using the arms to keep your balance.

3. If the ball is arriving to the left, use your left foot (and the same with the right).

4. A soft touch is needed to 'feel' when receiving, not to let the ball bounce off the foot.

5. The first touch should allow for the next action to be performed as easily as possible.

Variations

1. The players pretend there is a defender behind and take a directional first touch to the left or right.

2. Take an extra soft touch to keep the ball close to the feet, as if a defender was close by.

3. A heavier touch out in front for when there is plenty of space and time.

4. Sole or outside of the foot to receive, putting the standing leg between the ball and an 'opponent' behind.

Passing and Receiving in a 4 v 4 Small Sided Game with End Zones

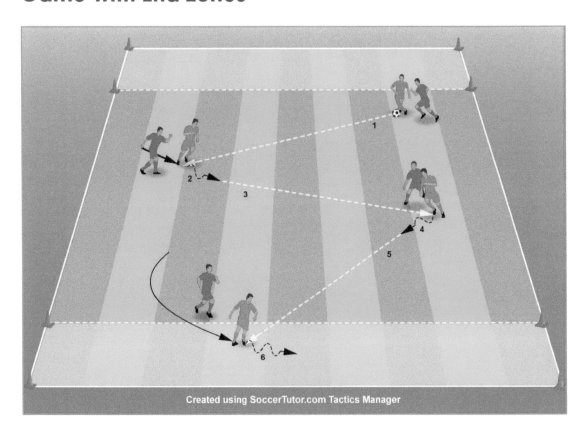

Created using SoccerTutor.com Tactics Manager

Objective

To develop the basic technique of receiving the ball and making a good directional first touch into space within a competitive small sided game. This practice also trains awareness and movement.

Description

In a 25 x 35 yard area, we play a 4v4 game with 2 end zones. The players practice passing and receiving in a competitive situation. A goal is scored when a player receives the ball from a teammate within the "end zone" and successfully takes it under control within the zone (under pressure from an opposition player).

Only one player on each team is allowed to enter the end zone at any given time.

Variation

Adjust the size of the area and you can play 2v2, 3v3, 5v5 or 6v6.

SESSION 2: THE SCISSOR

SESSION 2: The Scissor

Objective

To develop the technique to perform the scissor move.

Description

The "picture" says more than a long explanation. Demonstrate a good example of the proper technique to perform the scissor or let a technically skilled player demonstrate. Preferably demonstrate with a defender so the players can see how it works as a move to beat.

The scissor move is designed to make your opponent move one way and be wrong footed, so the attacker can then move the ball to the other side and pass the defender. The action is to step over the ball with one foot (in to out) pretending to move the ball one way with the outside of the foot, before then quickly taking the ball to the other side with the outside of the opposite foot.

Coaching Points

1. The step over should be done at a high speed.

2. Look over the ball to watch where the defender is and what he does.

3. Perform the movement at the right time. If it is too early, the defender can then recover. If it is too late, you will then get too close to the defender and they can intercept the ball.

4. Bend the knees before making the second movement away from the defender, then you can accelerate away with power.

5. When the defender moves with the feint, quickly touch the ball with the outside of the opposite foot to take it past the defender.

6. Make sure to always have control of the ball and do not make too heavy a touch.

7. Accelerate away from the defender with the ball so they have no time to recover.

Dutch Academy Football Coaching (U10-11)

Scissor Move and Awareness Exercise in a Big Space, then a Small Space

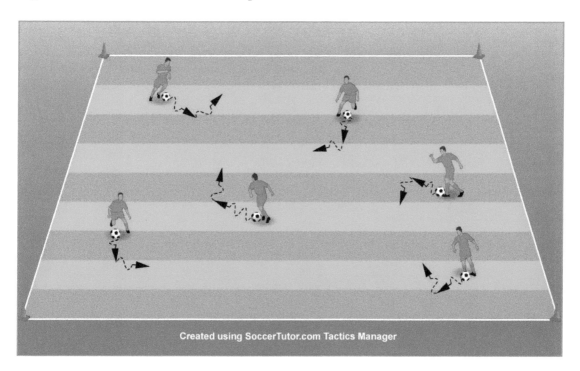

Created using SoccerTutor.com Tactics Manager

Objective

To develop the technique to perform the scissor as a move to beat in an open space.

Description

Everyone has their own ball and they practice performing the scissor move in a large space. The players should practice with both feet.

The players need to be aware of each other to avoid collisions and should also be aware of the space to move into with their second movement (as if away from a defender).

Progression

Use a small area (adjust the size of the area depending on the age/level of the players). In a small space, the emphasis is on the control of the ball after making the step over.

Variations

1. The players perform the movement on the command (or whistle) of the coach.

2. Perform a double scissor and then move away with the ball.

3. Add a second movement before or after the scissor to make it more complex.

The Scissor with Frontal Pressure

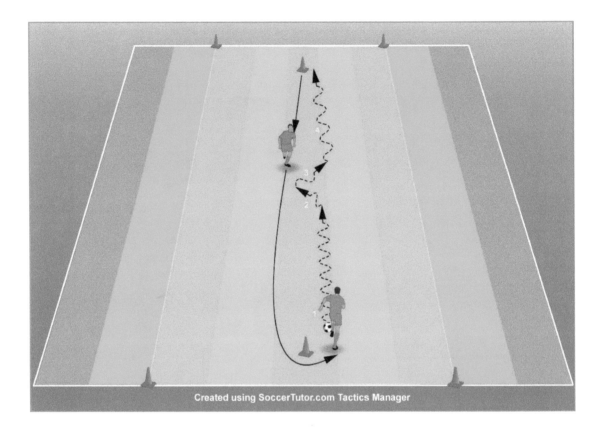

Created using SoccerTutor.com Tactics Manager

Objective

To practice the scissor as a move to beat with frontal pressure.

Description

The players are in pairs with one ball between them and stand approximately 15 yards apart. The first player runs forwards with the ball. The 'defender' applies passive pressure as the attacker performs a scissor to feint left and then takes the ball to the right with the outside of the right foot.

The attacker then dribbles the ball to the end and the defender runs to the opposite cone. The first player then passes the ball to the start position and the second player performs the same sequence. The practice continues this way.

Variations

1. The attacker uses a scissor to feint right and then takes the ball to the left with the outside of the left foot.

2. Add a small goal at one end so the players are able to score after they have beaten the defender.

42

The Scissor with Frontal Pressure (2)

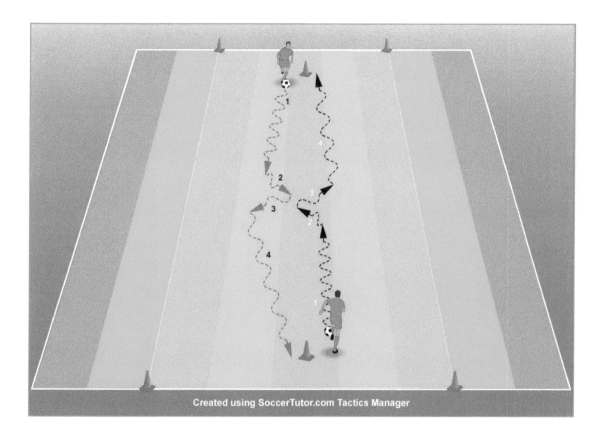

Created using SoccerTutor.com Tactics Manager

Objective

To practice the scissor move as a move to beat with frontal pressure.

Description

The players are in pairs and stand approximately 15 yards apart. Both players now have a ball each and run with the ball into the centre. Both players perform a scissor to feint left and then take the ball to the right with the outside of the right foot.

Variation

1. The players use a scissor to feint right and then take the ball to the left with the outside of the left foot.

2. Have all pairs working together and criss-cross in the penalty area.

Coaching Point

The players must be aware and look up, making the step over and movement at the right time with enough space, so they are careful not to collide with the other players.

The Scissor in a 1 v 1 Duel + Goalkeeper

Objective

To practice the scissor move as a move to beat with active frontal pressure and finishing.

Description

For this practice, we use a large goal in a 8 x 20 yard area split into 3 zones, but you can adjust the size of the area you use based on the age/level of the player. The two blue defenders alternate.

The attacker starts by dribbling the ball forwards towards the area marked with cones and the defender moves to apply pressure. The attacker makes a scissor move (step over) in one direction and then takes the ball in the opposite direction with the outside of the other foot. After going past the defender (who must stay within the coned area), the attacker dribbles forward and tries to score in the goal past the goalkeeper.

The defender starts as passive and progresses to half power, and finally to 100%.

Variations

1. You can remove the big goal with a goalkeeper and just have a small goal for the defender to defend.
2. Vary the task and get the attackers to combine different moves to beat.

The Scissor (and Moves to Beat) in a 5 v 5 Small Sided Game

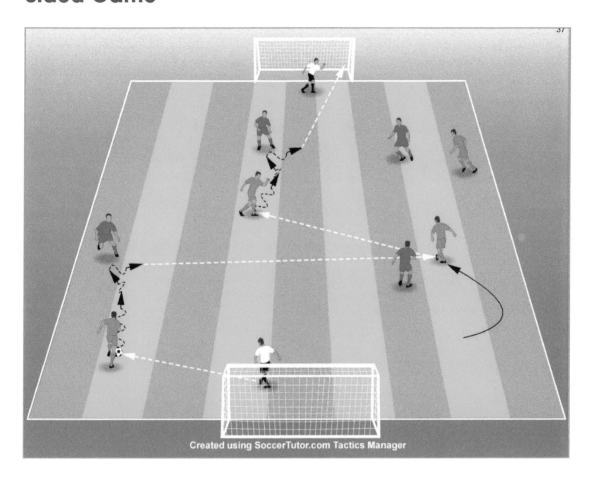

Created using SoccerTutor.com Tactics Manager

Objective

To practice the scissor as a move to beat within a competitive small sided game.

Description

We finish the session by playing a small sided game with large goals and goalkeepers.

Use a space large enough (adjust to age/level) so that the players have plenty of space to perform their move to beat. You can adjust the amount of players from 2v2, 3v3, 4v4, 6v6 etc.

If a player scores directly after a successful scissor move, the goal counts triple.

Variation

Vary the task and get the attackers to use and combine different moves to beat.

Dutch Academy Football Coaching (U10-11)

SESSION 3: THE 180° CHOP

SESSION 3: The 180° Chop

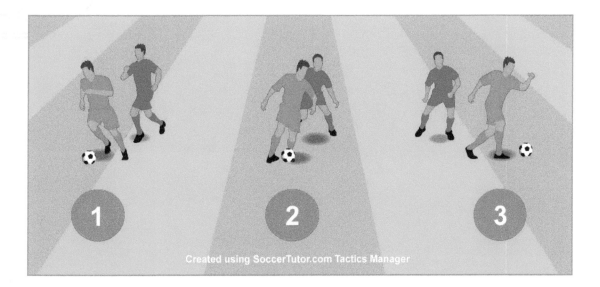

Created using SoccerTutor.com Tactics Manager

Objective

To develop the technique to perform the 180º chop move to take the ball at a horizontal angle away from the defender.

Description

The chop is used to turn 180º away e.g. To keep the ball in play near the sideline or shift the ball away from an oncoming opponent.

Having good ball control is very important so that there is a good feel of the ball. There are several similar movements which can have the same effect, but in this session we are only demonstrating the chop with the inside and the outside of the foot.

Demonstrate a good example of the proper technique to perform the chop or let a technically skilled player demonstrate. Preferably demonstrate with a defender so the players can see how it works as a move away from an opponent.

Coaching Points for the Chop with the Inside of the Foot

1. Make sure you are dribbling the ball under complete control with soft touches. Do not let the ball get too far away from your feet.

2. Put your standing leg right next to the ball and bend the knee so you are able to then move off quickly 180º in the opposite direction.

3. Shield the ball from the opponent and take a touch with the inside of the foot at a horizontal angle (across your body) to move away from the defender.

The 180° Chop Move and Awareness Exercise in a Big Space, then a Small Space

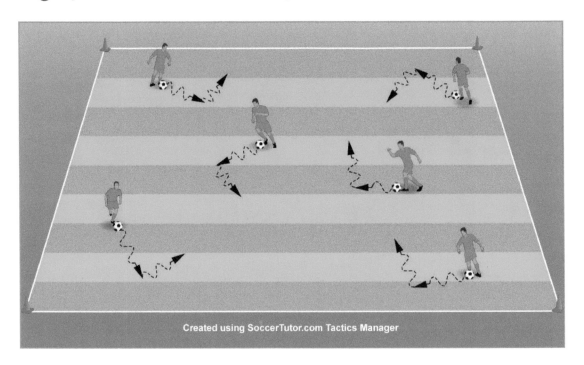

Created using SoccerTutor.com Tactics Manager

Objective

To develop the technique to perform the 180° chop move to move the ball away from a defender and into space.

Description

Everyone has their own ball and they practice performing the chop move in a large space (you can use the penalty area). The players should practice with both feet.

The players need to be aware of each other to avoid collisions and should also be aware of the space to move into (as if away from a defender).

Progression

Use a small area (adjust the size of the area depending on the age/level of the players). In a small space, the emphasis is on the control of the ball after making the chop move.

Variations

1. The players perform the movement on the command (or whistle) of the coach.

2. Have some players with the ball and some without. The 'defenders' approach the attackers who must then use the chop move to protect the ball and get away from them and into space.

The 180° Chop Practice in a Circle

Objective

To develop the technique to perform the 180º chop move within tight spaces.

Description

Make a circle with the same amount of cones as there are players. Adjust the size of the circle (3-5 yards) depending on the age/level of the players. A large cone or a player/coach stands in the middle.

The players all start with a ball next to an outside cone. They all dribble the ball towards the centre at the same time. When they reach the middle and approach the cone/defender, they then use the chop move (inside of the foot) to turn 180º and then dribble back to their outside cone.

Progression

Make it a continuous sequence where the players perform the chop move in the middle and at the outside cone.

Variations

1. Practice with both feet at the same time, e.g. chop move with the right foot in the centre and then a chop move with the left foot at the outside cone.

2. Turn the practice into a competition: Who can make the most successful chop moves in one minute?

3. If you have varying abilities, not everybody has to start at the same time, so some players can practice at their own pace.

4. Perform the chop move with the outside of the foot.

The 180° Chop in Pairs and Foursomes

Objective

To develop the technique to perform the 180° chop move to move the ball away from a defender and into space.

Description

In this practice we work with pairs and then with groups of 4.

Pairs: The 2 players stand approximately 15 yards apart and both players dribble a ball towards each other. As they meet each other in the middle, they both use the outside of their foot to move the ball horizontally 180° back in the direction they came from (to the start position).

Foursomes: We mark out a square with 4 cones. 2 players have a ball and the other 2 act as defenders. The 2 players with the ball start in opposite corners and both dribble to the right (change to left during practice).

The 2 defenders move off their cones to apply passive pressure to the ball carriers. The 2 ball carriers then perform a chop move with either the inside or outside of the foot, and return to their starting cone.

Change the roles of the players often.

The 180° Chop in a 1 v 1 Duel + Goalkeeper

Created using SoccerTutor.com Tactics Manager

Objective

To practice the 180º chop to move the ball away from a defender into space and finishing.

Description

In a 8 x 20 yard area, we mark out 3 zones as shown in the diagram. Adjust the size of the zones you use for this practice based on the age/level of the players. The two defenders alternate. The attacker starts by dribbling the ball forwards and the defender (who must stay within the central zone) moves to apply pressure for a 1v1 duel. The attacker dribbles the ball close to the defender, shields the ball with the standing leg and then uses the chop move to turn away at a horizontal angle. After going past the defender, the attacker dribbles forward and tries to score in the goal past the goalkeeper.

The defender starts as passive and progresses to half power, and finally to 100%. If the defender wins the ball, he can then try to score in the mini goal at the other end (and is now free to move across all zones).

Variations

1. You can remove the big goal with a goalkeeper and just have a small goal for the defender to defend.

2. Vary the task and get the attackers to use and combine different moves to beat.

The 180° Chop Move in a 4 v 4 Small Sided Game with End Zones

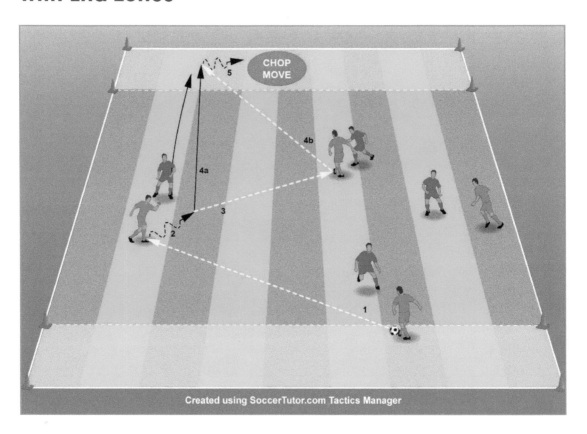

Created using SoccerTutor.com Tactics Manager

Objective

To practice the 180° chop within a competitive small sided game.

Description

In a 20 x 40 yard area, we play a 4v4 game. The aim is to work the ball to a teammate who moves to receive in the end zone. That player must then be aware of an oncoming defender and perform a chop move within the end zone to score a goal. Only one player from each team is allowed in the end zone at any given time.

Variation

You can vary the size of the end zone from large to small. With a small end zone, the pressure will be greater (less time for the ball carrier who is under pressure from their direct opponent).

Coaching Point

The weight and timing of the final pass is important because the attacker will usually make the final run in behind at high speed into the end zone and will most likely have a defender within close proximity.

SESSION 4: THE CHOP BACK HEEL

Session 4: The Chop Back Heel

SESSION 4: The Chop Back Heel

Objective

To develop the technique to perform the back heel chop to take the ball away from a defender.

Description

The chop back heel is used as a feint and to turn away from an opponent. The players practice with both feet.

The back heel chop can also be used as a 'Fake Shot' to commit the defender and then take the ball away from them. The back heel chop is of course not an end in itself, but works to create space for the next action. In the practices to follow it is just an end in itself, but the players have to understand why it is useful in a game situation.

Demonstrate a good example of the proper technique to perform the back heel chop or let a technically skilled player demonstrate. Preferably demonstrate with a defender so the players can see how it works as a move away from an opponent.

Coaching Points for Back Heel Chop (Right Foot)

1. Dribble the ball under control with your right foot and look up to see where your opponent is.

2. Make one last big step and plant your standing leg (left) beyond the ball. Your left leg should be slightly twisted outwards because you will soon be turning to that side.

3. Bend your left knee so the next movement can be as quick as possible.

4. Bend the right knee and lift the left up, covering the ball with your right foot back. Then use the inside of the right foot to take the ball away at a 90° angle to the left.

5. Turn around and make sure you immediately have control of the ball.

©SoccerTutor.com   54   Dutch Academy Football Coaching (U10-11)

The Chop Back Heel and Awareness Exercise in a Big Space, then a Small Space

Objective

To develop the technique to perform the back heel chop to take the ball away from a defender.

Description

Everyone has their own ball and they practice performing the back heel chop in a large space (you can use the penalty area). The players should practice with both feet.

The players need to be aware of each other to avoid collisions and should also be aware of the space to move into (as if away from a defender).

Progression

Use a small area (adjust the size of the area depending on the age/level of the players). In a small space, the emphasis is on the control of the ball after making the back heel chop.

Variations

1. The players perform the movement on the command (or whistle) of the coach.

2. Have some players with the ball and some without. The 'defenders' approach the attackers who must then use the chop move to protect the ball and get away from them and into space.

3. Alternate with other moves to beat that have been learnt.

The Chop Back Heel in a Continuous Dribbling Circle Exercise

Created using SoccerTutor.com Tactics Manager

Objective

To develop the technique to perform the back heel chop within tight spaces with passive pressure.

Description

In this practice, we play with 12 players. Make a circle using 6 cones with a diameter of approximately 15 yards. On each cone there is a player without a ball (blue). In between each two cones is a player with a ball (orange).

The players with the ball start at the same time and aim to dribble to one of their teammate's positions ('home'). They do not have to dribble to the position directly opposite, but can dribble to any of the 5 possible positions.

As an orange player approaches 'home', one of the blue players then moves off their cone to contest them in a passive way. The orange player must go past the defender (using the chop back heel) and then dribble 'home'. Swap the roles of the players every minute.

Variation: Increase or decrease the diameter of the circle to vary the difficulty level.

Dutch Academy Football Coaching (U10-11)

The Chop Back Heel in a Circle Dribbling Game

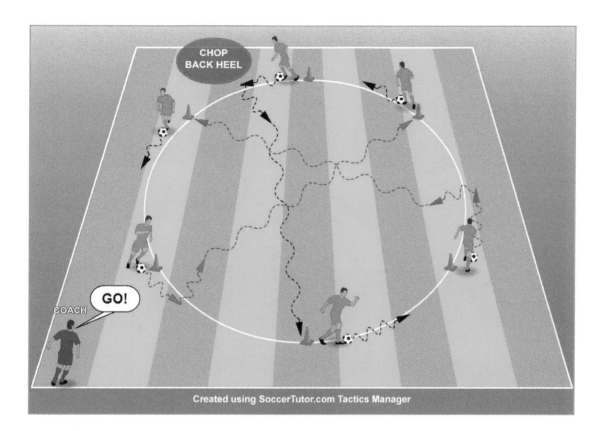

Created using SoccerTutor.com Tactics Manager

Objective

To develop the technique to perform the back heel chop within tight spaces and dribbling/running with the ball.

Description

We work with 6 players and mark out a circle with 6 cones. All players have a ball and dribble around the edge of the circle. When the coach gives the signal, all the players perform a back heel chop into the circle and then dribble the ball to a cone on the opposite side.

Adjust the distances and space in these types of practices to the age/level of the players.

Coaching Points

1. In a small space, the emphasis is on the control of the ball after making the back heel chop.

2. The back heel chop should be performed at a high pace, as if away from a defender in a game.

3. The players need to look up and be aware so they keep control of the ball and avoid collisions with teammates.

The Chop Back Heel in a 4 v 4 Small Sided Game with End Zones

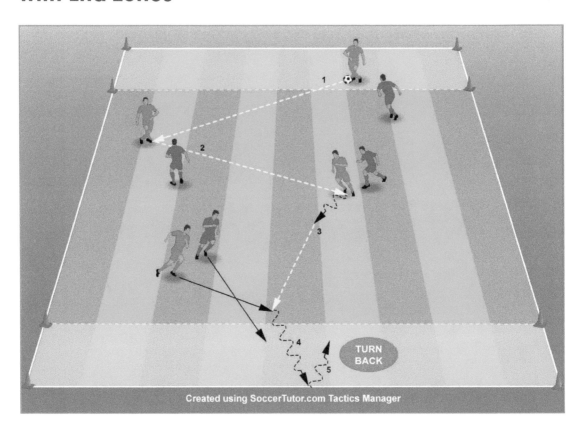

Created using SoccerTutor.com Tactics Manager

Objective

To develop the technique to perform the back heel chop within a competitive small sided game.

Description

In a 20 x 40 yard area, we play a 4v4 game. The aim is to first dribble the ball past the line. That player must then be aware of an oncoming defender and perform a back heel chop within the end zone to score a goal.

Only one player from each team can enter the end zone at any given time.

Variations

1. You can vary the size of the end zone from large to small. With a small end zone, the pressure will be greater (less time for the ball carrier under pressure from the defender in the end zone).

2. You can choose to make the area wider or longer, depending on your requirements.

3. This game can also be 1v1, 2v2, 3v3 etc.

SESSION 5: 90° TURN

SESSION 5: 90° Turn

Objective

To develop the technique to perform the 90° turn away from a defender.

Description

A 90° movement is somewhere between a chop and a trick. This movement can be performed by any player in any position on the pitch e.g. if you want to avoid an opponent, if you want to make a pass in a different direction or to keep the ball in play near the sideline.

The ball can be rolled back with the sole, but also cut with the inside or outside of the foot. The is determined by the situation and the preference of the player to determine what best suits them.

A 90° turn is often combined with a feint, which knocks the opponent off balance and at that time you touch the ball towards the other side away from the defender.

Have the demonstration with a defender, allowing the players to see how the movement is effective to beat an opponent.

Coaching Points (Sole and Outside of Foot Touch)

1. Dribble the ball under control and do not let the ball go too far away from your feet (soft touches).

2. Look where your opponent is and what he does (this determines the timing of the movement).

3. Roll the ball back with the sole away from the opponent and to the side.

4. The left foot stays planted and the right foot moves back with the ball to create an open body shape.

5. Keep your body between the ball and the opponent and use your arms to keep your balance. Then touch the ball with the outside of the right foot away from the defender.

6. Make sure you have direct control over the ball again and you can dribble away at speed.

90° Turns and Awareness Exercise in a Big Space, then a Small Space

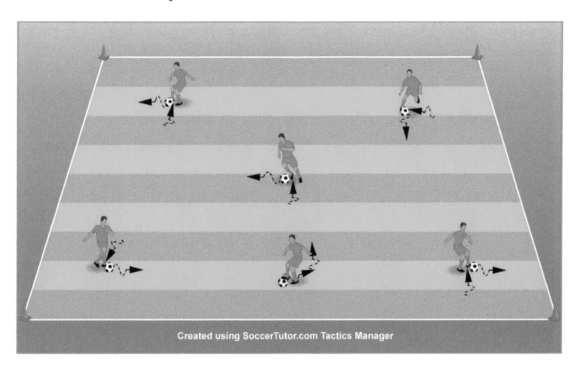

Created using SoccerTutor.com Tactics Manager

Objective

To develop the technique to perform the 90° turn away from a defender.

Description

Everyone has their own ball and they practice performing the 90° turn in a large space (you can use the penalty area). The players should practice with both feet. The correct technical execution is very important. The players need to be aware of each other to avoid collisions and should also be aware of the space to move into (as if away from a defender).

Progression

Use a small area (adjust the size of the area depending on the age/level of the players). In a small space, the emphasis is on the control of the ball after making the 90° turn.

Variations

1. The players perform the movement on the command (or whistle) of the coach.

2. Have some players with the ball and some without. The 'defenders' approach the attackers who must then use the 90° turn to protect the ball and get away from them and into space.

3. Make it a competition to see how many successful 90° turns the players can make in 30 seconds.

90° Turns in a Dribbling Circuit

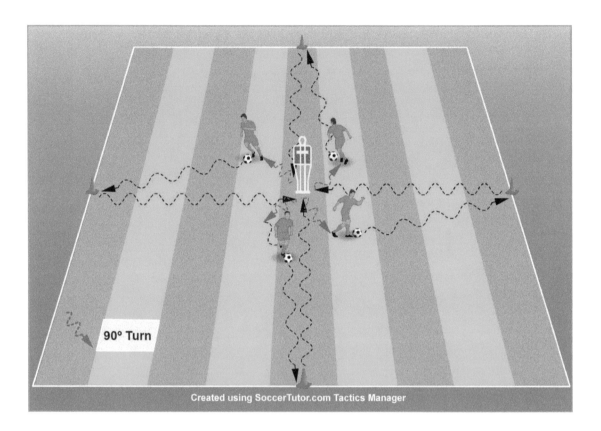

90° Turn

Created using SoccerTutor.com Tactics Manager

Objective

To develop the technique to perform the 90° turn within tight spaces.

Description

We mark out 5 cones as shown with 1 player on each of the 4 outside cones. Adjust the size of the circle depending on the age/level of the players.

The players all start with a ball and dribble the ball towards the centre at the same time. When they reach the middle and approach the cone, they then use the 90° turn (roll the ball back away from the cone and turn to the right) and dribble to the next cone.

Variation

Change the direction (clockwise or anti-clockwise) which will also change which foot is used (right -> left).

90° Turns in a Square Dribbling Exercise

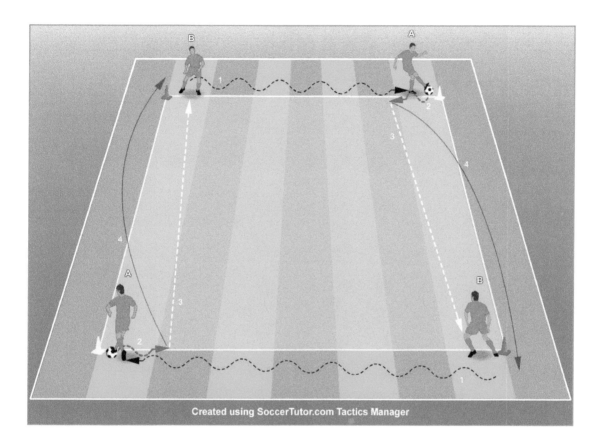

Created using SoccerTutor.com Tactics Manager

Objective

To develop the technique to perform the 90º turn within tight spaces.

Description

In a 5 x 5 yard square we have 4 players and 2 balls. Adjust the size of the area depending on the age/level of the players. We have 2 Player A's who start from opposite corners (red cones) and 2 cones are left free (yellow).

The 2 Player A's start the practice by dribbling in opposite directions towards the yellow cones. Once they reach the yellow cone, they then use the 90º turn (roll the ball back away from the cone and turn to the right). After that, they pass to the player to the right of them (Player B on the red cone). Both Player B's (who receive the passes) repeat the same sequence and the Player A's move to the next cone in a clockwise direction.

Variations

1. Change the direction (clockwise or anti-clockwise) so the players use both feet for all parts.

2. Add a one-two combination to the sequence.

Dutch Academy Football Coaching (U10-11)

90° Turns in a 2 v 2 Duel Game

Created using SoccerTutor.com Tactics Manager

Objective

To develop the technique to perform the 90º turn with competitive duels.

Description

In a 15 x 20 yard area, we play a 2v2 duel game with small goals (1-2 yards wide). When coaching during this game, it is important to stimulate the creation of functional 90° movements.

One team starts with 2 balls and each ball carrier tries to beat their direct opponent and then score in the goal. If a defender (blues in diagram) wins the ball, they then quickly to try to score in the goal at the opposite end.

If a player scores a goal directly after using a 90° movement, then the goal is worth triple.

Variations

1. Play with 3 teams. The third pair rests when not playing or can referee the game.

2. This duel game can also be simplified to 1v1.

90° Turns in a 5 v 5 Small Sided Game

Created using SoccerTutor.com Tactics Manager

Objective

To develop the technique to perform the 90° turn within a competitive small sided game.

Description

In a 25 x 35 yard area, we play a 5v5 game with large goals. When coaching during this game, it is important to stimulate the creation of functional 90° movements.

If a player scores a goal directly after using a 90° movement, then the goal is worth triple.

Variations

1. Adjust the size of the area depending on the age/level and number of players.

2. Play with small goals and without goalkeepers.

SESSION 6: THE ELASTIC DRAG (OR FLIP FLAP)

SESSION 6: The Elastic Drag (or Flip Flap)

Description

The elastic drag move is meant to unbalance your opponent so you can then go past him. The player feints to go one way with the first touch with the inside of the foot, then suddenly uses the outside of the same foot to move the ball the other way and past the defender.

Have the demonstration with a defender, allowing the players to see how the movement is effective to beat an opponent.

Coaching Points (Right Foot)

1. Dribble the ball with complete control using your strongest foot.

2. Look where your opponent is.

3. Start the movement approximately 5 yards away from the opponent.

4. Drag the ball with the inside of the right foot to the left, drop the left shoulder and bend the left leg. Retain contact with the ball.

5. Feint to beat your opponent to your left (their right side).

6. When the opponent moves with the feint, you then use the outside of the right foot (still retaining contact with the ball) to move the ball in the opposite direction (towards the right) and beat the opponent.

7. Bend your left knee so you can then make an explosive movement away from the opponent.

8. Dribble away at speed, allowing your opponent no chance to recover.

The Elastic Drag Move and Awareness Exercise in a Big Space, then a Small Space

Objective

To develop the technique to perform the elastic drag move away from a defender.

Description

Everyone has their own ball and they practice performing the elastic drag move in a large space (you can use the penalty area). The players should practice with both feet. The correct technical execution is very important.

The players need to be aware of each other to avoid collisions and should also be aware of the space to move into (as if away from a defender).

Progression

Use a small area (adjust the size of the area depending on the age/level of the players). In a small space, the emphasis is on the control of the ball after making the drag move.

Variations

1. The players perform the movement on the command (or whistle) of the coach.

2. Have some players with the ball and some without. The 'defenders' approach the attackers who must then use the drag move to protect the ball and get away from them and into space.

3. Make it a competition to see how many successful drag moves the players can make in 30 seconds.

The Elastic Drag Move in a Continuous Dribbling Circuit

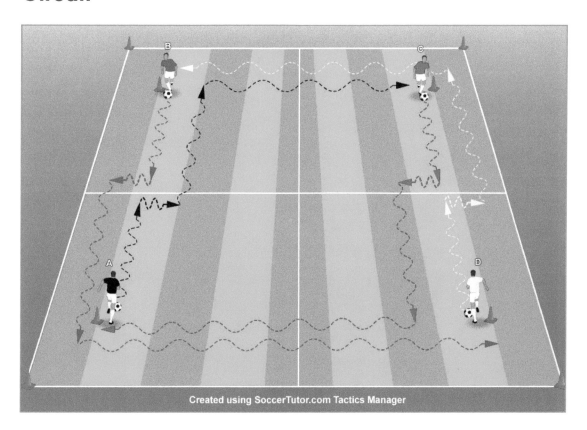

Created using SoccerTutor.com Tactics Manager

Objective

To develop the technique to perform the elastic drag while dribbling at speed (with passive frontal resistance).

Description

In a 20 x 20 yard area, each player starts on one cone with a ball. Two players (A and B / C and D) vertical to each other, work together so they reach the middle at the same time. When they meet in the middle, they both perform the elastic drag move (feint left and go right).

Each player's path is shown by their specific colour in the diagram. It is important that every time the players are moving to be opposite again, they are aware that they should dribble from the cone at the exact same time.

Variations

1. Change direction with an anti-clockwise rotation, with the players using their left foot for the elastic drag.
2. This practice can be carried out with up to 8 players.
3. Change the sequence to include a diagonal dribble, with players being careful not to collide.

The Elastic Drag Move in a Dynamic Competitive Duel Practice

Created using SoccerTutor.com Tactics Manager

Objective

To develop the technique to perform the elastic drag move away from a defender in a competitive duel.

Description

In a 8 x 20 yard area, we mark out 3 zones as shown in the diagram. Adjust the size of the zones you use for this practice based on the age/level of the players. The attacker dribbles the ball forwards into the central zone and then attempts to beat the oncoming defender. Encourage the use of the elastic drag in this situation.

To make sure the defender is not easily able to predict the movement, the attacker may also play a one-two combination with the other attacker positioned to one side (this player is limited to one touch only).

After beating the defender, the attacker then dribbles the ball into the penalty area and tries to score in the goal past the goalkeeper. If the defender wins the ball, he tries to score in the 2 mini goals at the opposite end.

Variations

1. Adapt for a 2v2 duel practice.
2. Change the angle and depth of the defender to vary the point of attack with different situations to overcome.

The Elastic Drag Move in Continuous 1 v 1 Duels

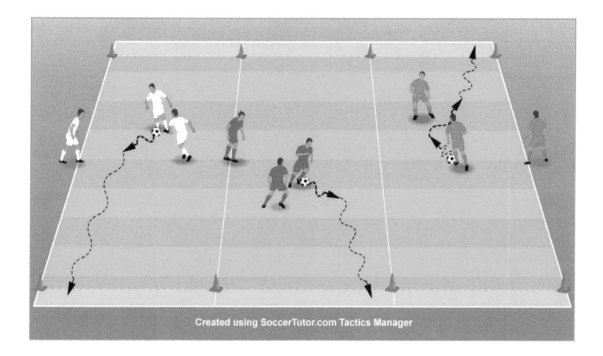

Created using SoccerTutor.com Tactics Manager

Objective

To develop the technique to perform the drag move away from a defender in a competitive duel.

Description

In a 5 x 20 yard area, the players work in groups of 3. Within each group, 2 of the players compete in a 1v1 duel and the third player rests and referees.

At each end, there is a line with the aim to dribble past it to score a goal. The players compete in a 1v1 duel, with the focus to use moves to beat to dribble the ball past their opponent. A goal counts triple if the elastic drag move is used successfully before dribbling across the end line.

Make sure as a coach that you keep an eye on the work to rest ratio. The recommended ratio is to have one and half minutes action, followed by a one minute rest.

Variations

1. Use a competitive tournament format.

2. Add small goals for the players to score in after beating their opponent.

3. Adapt for a 2v2 duel practice.

SESSION 7: THE 'V' MOVE

SESSION 7: The 'V' Move

Description

The V-move is named as such because of the path the ball travels. The movement is particularly suited to beating an opponent (or turning) to open up play in another direction. The players should practice using both feet and in both directions.

The player dribbles the ball and feints to go in one direction, then drags the ball back towards themselves, before touching the ball in the other direction to either dribble away or pass towards the other side.

This move is often used when one side of the pitch is congested and this allows for the player to create space and switch the play.

Coaching Points

1. Dribble the ball to one side, in this example to the left.

2. Place your right foot on the ball and roll it towards yourself with the sole of the foot.

3. Open up your body to the right using your hip.

4. Take the ball with the inside (or outside) of the foot in the other direction and accelerate away.

5. This movement creates space for the player and the next action can be to dribble, pass or even shoot at goal in some situations.

The 'V' Move and Passing Exercise in Pairs

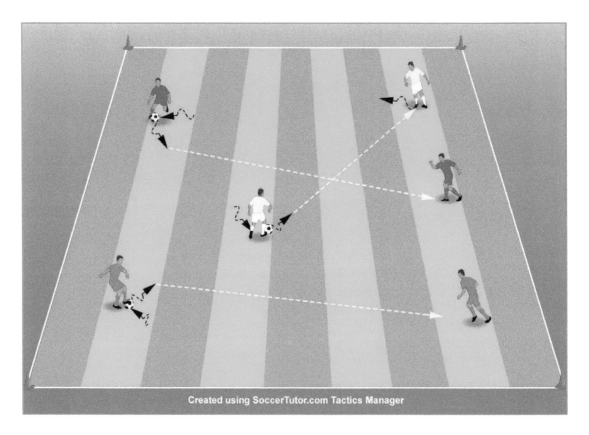

Created using SoccerTutor.com Tactics Manager

Objective

To develop the technique to perform the 'V' move away from a defender, with passing and receiving.

Description

With one ball between each pair, the players practice performing the 'V' move in a large space (you can use the penalty area). The players should practice with both feet. The correct technical execution is very important.

After completing the movement, the player then passes to their teammate, who receives and does the same. The players need to be aware of each other to avoid collisions and should also be aware of the space to move into (as if away from a defender).

Progressions

1. Use a small area with less pairs (adjust the size of the area depending on the age/level of the players).

2. The players still work in pairs, but this time apply pressure to each other so the ball carrier can practice the 'V' movement in a competitive situation. The 'defenders' approach the attackers who must then use the 'V' move to protect the ball and get away from them and into space.

    Dutch Academy Football Coaching (U10-11)

Moves to Beat in a Dynamic 4 Goal Duel Practice

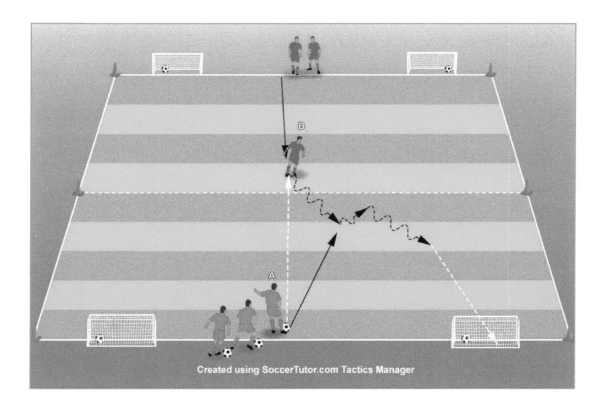

Created using SoccerTutor.com Tactics Manager

Objective

To practice moves to beat in competitive duels with finishing.

Description

In a 10 x 20 yard area we mark out 2 equal zones and position 4 mini goals on the outside as shown in the diagram.

Player A starts the practice and passes the ball to player B, then moves forwards to apply pressure. Player B must dribble past the halfway line and use a move to beat and try to score in either of the 2 mini goals. If a 'V' move is used successfully before scoring, the goal counts triple. The next 2 players then continue in the same way.

Variations

1. Allow Player B to score in the mini goal without having to perform a move to beat or cross the halfway line.

2. A goal is scored by dribbling the ball into the mini goal (or between 2 cones or boundary poles).

Moves to Beat in a Dynamic 1 v 1 Duel Practice

Created using SoccerTutor.com Tactics Manager

Objective

To practice moves to beat in competitive duels with finishing.

Description

In a 10 x 20 yard area, we can play with up to 12 players for this practice. Adjust the size of the area to the age/level of your players. We have a small goal at each end as shown in the diagram.

Player A starts the practice by dribbling the ball forwards, performing a technical movement (move to beat i.e. the 'V' move) to change direction and then shoots in the goal. He then runs around the goal to the opposite side as shown in the diagram.

Player B then passes the ball to Player A, who plays a one touch pass into B's path so he can run onto it. Player B then faces Player A (who becomes a defender) in a 1v1 duel and tries to score in the goal. If Player A wins the ball, he can then score in the small goal at the other end.

As soon as a goal is scored or the ball goes out of play, the next blue player starts the same sequence.

SESSION 8: THE TRAIN (STOP & GO)

SESSION 8: The Train (Stop & Go)

Description

The Train is used when an opponent may be close behind you or next to you. It is often used to create space near to the flank so the player can deliver a cross. The Train movement takes its name from the way the player's leg bends at the knee, moving the ball forwards just like a train.

The players should practice using both feet and in both directions.

The player dribbles the ball, slows down/stops with the sole of the foot and then dribbles forwards again into space, leaving the defender behind.

Coaching Points

1. Dribble forwards and keep the ball close to the feet.

2. Keep the ball away from the opponent using the outside of the foot.

3. Slow down and place the sole of your foot on the ball.

4. The opponent responds by slowing or even stopping. At that time you accelerate quickly forwards.

5. Try to cut across the defender, leaving him no angle or room to recover.

Variations

1. Stop the ball completely or even roll it slightly back to feint as if you are turning backwards. Then you accelerate quickly forwards again.

2. The movement is also very useful when parallel to the edge of the penalty area. You can use it to create a yard of space to lose an opponent and shoot at goal.

The Train Move (Stop & Go) Dribbling Exercise

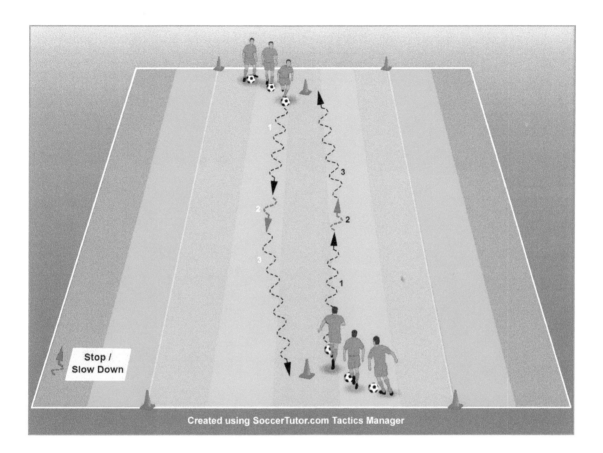

Stop /
Slow Down

Created using SoccerTutor.com Tactics Manager

Objective

To develop the technique to perform the Train move (slow down/stop and then accelerate) to create space and get away from a defender.

Description

We work in groups with 2 cones 15-20 yards apart. 2 players start from 2 sides simultaneously and dribble the ball forwards. At the moment when they pass each other, they make the Train movement. Switch the sides the players start from halfway through so they practice with their left foot too.

Coaching Points

1. The ball must be dribbled forwards with the outside of the foot, as if to keep the ball away from an opponent (using the body as a barrier between the defender and the ball).

2. The key parts of this practice are the level of control when dribbling and the timing of the action.

The Train Move 1 v 1 Duel: Create Space and Shoot from the Edge of the Penalty Area

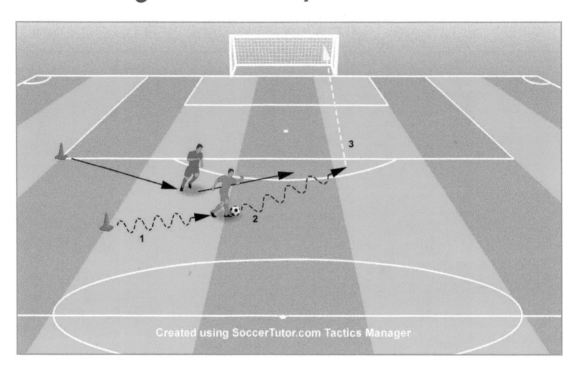

Created using SoccerTutor.com Tactics Manager

Objective

To develop the technique to perform the Train move (slow down/stop and then accelerate) to create space on the edge of the penalty area and shooting.

Description

The two players start next to the cones as shown in the diagram. The orange player with the ball dribbles across the 18 yard line and is put under pressure by the blue defender who starts off as passive, then at half power and finally defends with 100% competitiveness.

The attacker must shoot from within the width of the penalty box and outside of it. The aim is for the attacker to dribble with the ball using feints and with stop/start actions.

Encourage the use of the train movement to feint and then accelerate away from the defender to create space and shoot at goal.

Variation

You can add a mini goal near the halfway line. If the defender wins the ball, he then tries to score himself.

The Train Move, Crossing and Finishing in a 7 v 7 Small Sided Game with Side Zones

Created using SoccerTutor.com Tactics Manager

Objective

To develop the technique to perform the Train move (slow down/stop and then accelerate) within a competitive small sided game, with crossing and finishing.

Description

Using half a pitch, we play a 7v7 small sided game. We mark out 2 side zones as shown in the diagram. In each side zone, there is a 1v1 situation and no other players are allowed to enter these zones.

The players in the centre aim to pass the ball out wide. The player in the side zone must then try to beat the defender (preferably using the Train move) and then dribble forwards and cross the ball into the penalty area.

The players in the centre time their runs forward to try and score past the goalkeeper.

SESSION 9: HIP FEINT AND CHANGE DIRECTION

SESSION 9: Hip Feint and Change Direction

Description

This hip feint movement is used when a player has their back to their opponent. The player uses the hip feint and change direction move to feint in one direction and put the defender off balance, before turning in the opposite direction and accelerating away with the ball.

This movement is particularly suitable for when an attacker has their back to goal around the penalty area. With this one action a player can unlock themselves (create space) and shoot at goal or give the final pass.

Coaching Points

1. Know where your opponent is, and possibly make contact.
2. Keep the defender behind you (shield the ball).
3. Have full control of the ball.
4. Turn your hip in, with the knee slightly bent, as if you're going to shoot.
5. Feint to hit the ball, and then turn in the opposite direction.
6. Take the ball onto the other foot (inside of the foot) and move away from the defender.
7. Accelerate away with the ball and cut across the defender so they do not have the angle or time to recover.

Variations

1. Double hip feint and change direction.
2. Take the touch away using the outside of the foot.

1 v 1 Duel and Dribbling Circuit

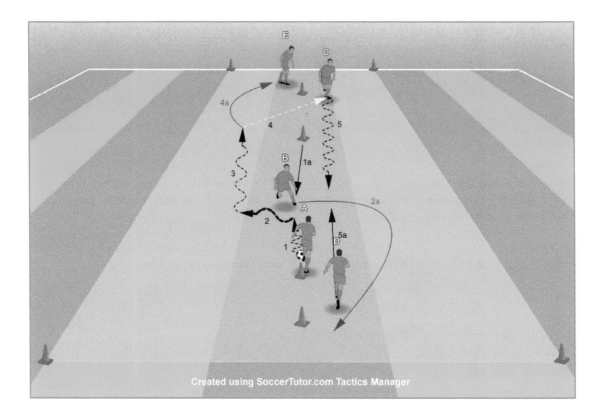

Created using SoccerTutor.com Tactics Manager

Objective

To develop the technique to perform moves to beat in a dribbling exercise.

Description

In a 10 x 20 yard area, we work with groups of 5 players.

Player A starts the practice by dribbling the ball forwards. Player B moves to contest him (passively) and Player A then performs a move to beat and dribbles the ball past B. To complete the first part of the sequence, Player A passes to Player C and moves into a position behind E. Player B moves into a position behind D.

Player C then starts the same sequence again by dribbling the ball forwards. Player D is the player to move forward and contest him as the sequence continues in the same way, but in the opposite direction.

The players who apply pressure on the ball carriers (B and D in the diagram example) start off as passive, then move to half power and finally defend with 100% competitiveness.

CHAPTER 8

POSITIONAL GAMES WITH A NUMERICAL ADVANTAGE

Positional 3 v 1 Possession Exercise

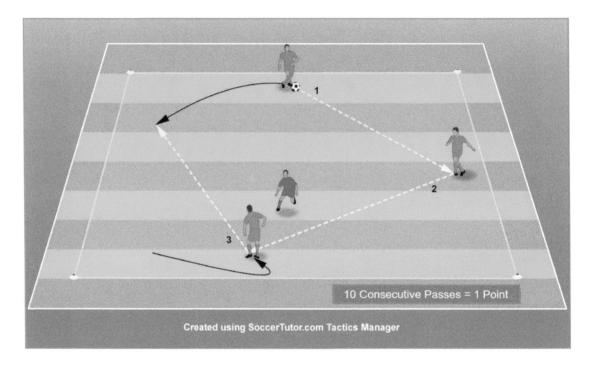

10 Consecutive Passes = 1 Point

Created using SoccerTutor.com Tactics Manager

Objective

To develop passing, possession, player movement and collective defending.

Description

We work with 4 players in a 7 x 10 yard area (or 10 x 12) in a possession exercise. The attackers (orange) score 1 point if they are able to complete 10 successful consecutive passes.

If the fully active defender (blue) wins the ball and gets it under full control or kicks/dribbles the ball out of the area he scores 1 point. Once the defender wins 3 points, he switches roles with one of the attackers.

Variations

1. To make the practice harder for the attackers, reduce the width and/or length of the area.
2. To make the practice harder for the defender, increase the width and/or length of the area.

Coaching Points for Maintaining Possession

1. This practice is used to develop the ability to keep the ball (playing together to maintain possession).
2. The players must use actions with the ball under levels of resistance (space, time, opposition pressure etc).
3. The players learn how to keep the game moving under pressure from a defender.

4. The introduction of a defender forces the players in possession to make more mistakes, so they must learn to make quick and correct decisions to avoid this.

5. The weight of the passes is key so their teammates can receive easily and then pass again.

6. Monitor the positioning of the players and their movement into space, making sure they provide the right angles to receive the next pass.

Coaching Points for the Defender

1. The defender learns to position themselves in a certain way so they are able to block potential passes and intercept the ball (the correct body shape can be demonstrated for this).

2. The defenders start to learn and understand the right time to attack the ball and try to win it.

Positional 5 v 2 Possession Exercise

10 Consecutive Passes = 1 Point   Win the ball = 1 Point

Created using SoccerTutor.com Tactics Manager

Description

We work with 8 players in a 10 x 25 yard area (or 15 x 30) in a possession exercise. The attackers (orange) score 1 point if they are able to complete 10 successful consecutive passes.

If the fully active defenders (blue) win the ball and get it under full control or kick/dribble the ball out of the area they score 1 point. Once the defenders score 3 points, they switch roles with 3 of the attackers.

Variations

1. To make the practice harder for the attackers, reduce the width and/or length of the area.
2. To make the practice harder for the defender, increase the width and/or length of the area.

Coaching Points

The coaching points are the same as the previous practice, but the 3 defenders now need to work together, making sure to keep close to each other reducing the size of the gaps (angles and positioning are key).

Positional 4 v 2 Possession Exercise

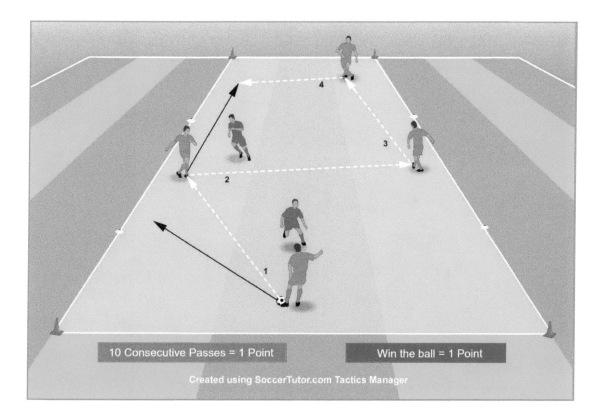

10 Consecutive Passes = 1 Point   Win the ball = 1 Point

Created using SoccerTutor.com Tactics Manager

Objective

To develop passing, possession, player movement and collective defending.

Description

We work with 6 players in an 8 x 18 yard area (or 15 x 22) in a possession exercise.

The attackers (orange) score 1 point if they are able to complete 10 successful consecutive passes.

If the fully active defenders (blue) win the ball and get it under full control or kick/dribble the ball out of the area they score 1 point. Once the defenders score 3 points, they switch roles with 2 of the attackers.

2 v 1 Dynamic Positional 2 Zone Game with Goalkeepers

Description

In a 12 x 30 yard area, we have 2 attackers (orange), 1 defender (blue), 2 goalkeepers and 2 large goals. The width and length of the area can be changed depending on whether the attackers play alongside or behind each other.

The practice either starts with the orange team's goalkeeper or with an orange player in the corner. The attackers aim to beat the blue defender and then score in the big goal.

If the defender wins the ball, he can then try to score in the goal at the opposite end (which counts as 2 goals). Change the player roles often.

Variations

1. To make the practice harder for the attackers, reduce the width of the area.

2. To make the practice harder for the defender, increase the width of the area.

3. The defender scores an extra point if he is able to win the ball in his half and then score.

4. Play with the offside rule - to make it simpler you can create an offside line 15 yards from goal.

Coaching Points for the 2 Attackers

1. The attacking players should try to score as quickly as possible. If a player is in space, he should take the opportunity to shoot at goal.

2. There needs to be good movement with and without the ball to create space and scoring opportunities.

3. The players should be aware of their teammate and pass to them if they are in a better position. This practice starts to develop 'playmaking'.

4. If the goalkeeper collects/saves the ball, he should then pass quickly to continue the game.

5. Encourage the players to use feints/moves to beat they have learnt to unbalance the defender and quickly move the ball in the opposite direction.

6. The accuracy and weight of the passes is key to success in this practice.

Coaching Points for the Defender

1. The positional play is very important, so the defender learns to defend his goal and prevent passes in behind.

2. When applying pressure, it is important to force the ball carrier to one side (side-on body shape).

3. Timing the right moment to move forward to try to steal the ball is key.

4. Try to prevent shots on goal and get in position to block shots.

5. Do not retreat towards your own goal.

6. Communicate with the goalkeeper and work together to defend.

2 v 1 Dynamic Positional Game with 3 Goals

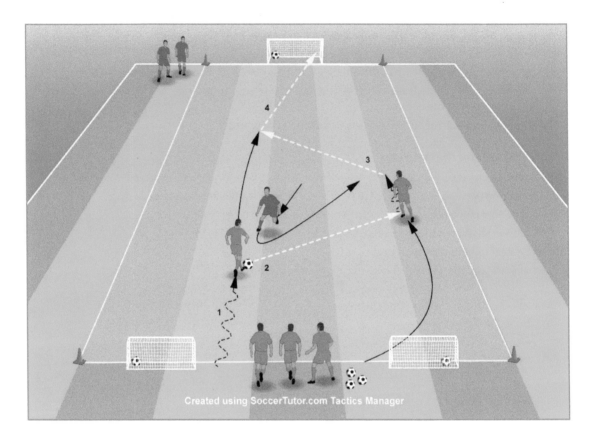

Description

In a 10 x 20 yard area, we have 5 attackers (orange) and 3 defenders (blue). The size of the area can be changed depending on the age/level of the players. We play 2v1 duels and the other players wait on the outside. There is 1 small goal at one end and 2 small goals at the other end.

The practice starts with an orange player dribbling the ball forward from in between the 2 goals. The attackers aim to beat the defender and then score a goal. If the defender wins the ball, he can then try to score in one of the 2 goals at the opposite end (which counts as 2 goals).

If a goal is scored or the ball goes out of play, the players leave and the next 2 orange players and the next blue player enter to repeat the same 2v1 duel. Change the player roles after a predetermined period of time.

Variations

1. To make the practice harder for the attackers, reduce the width of the area.
2. Play with the offside rule - to make it simpler you can create an offside line 10 yards from goal.

Coaching Points for the 2 Attackers

1. The players need to occupy good positions on the field to provide passing angles.

2. There needs to be good movement with and without the ball to create space and scoring opportunities.

3. The accuracy and weight of the passes is key to success in this practice.

4. When receiving a pass, the first touch should be quick and be out of the feet so they can shoot quickly, not allowing the defender time to recover.

5. Encourage the players to use feints/moves to beat they have learnt to unbalance the defender and quickly move the ball in the opposite directions.

Coaching Points for the Defender

1. The positional play is very important, so the defender learns to defend his goal and prevent passes in behind.

2. Timing the right moment to move forward to try to steal the ball is key.

3. Actively defend, preventing shots on goal and getting in position to block shots.

Positional 5 v 3 Posession Game

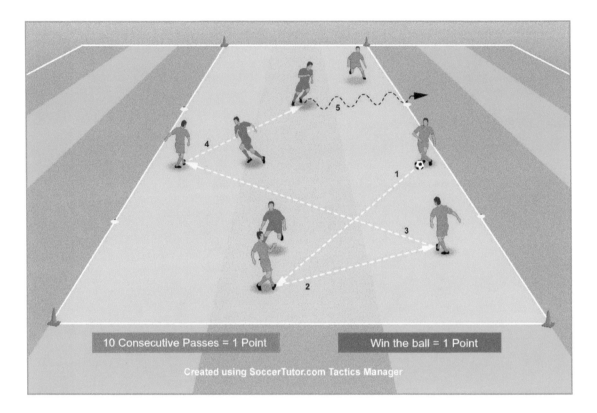

10 Consecutive Passes = 1 Point   Win the ball = 1 Point

Created using SoccerTutor.com Tactics Manager

Objective

To develop passing, possession, player movement and collective defending.

Description

We work with 8 players in an 8 x 25 yard area in a possession exercise. The attackers (orange) score 1 point if they are able to complete 10 successful consecutive passes. If the defenders (blue) win the ball and get it under full control, dribble the ball out the short side or kick the ball out of the area, they score 1 point. Once the defenders score 3 points, they switch roles with 3 of the attackers.

Variations

1. To make the practice harder for the attackers, reduce the width and/or length of the area.
2. To make the practice harder for the defenders, increase the width and/or length of the area.

Coaching Points for Maintaining Possession

1. This practice is used to develop the ability to keep the ball (playing together to maintain possession).
2. The players must use actions with the ball under levels of resistance (space, time, opposition pressure etc).

3. The players learn how to keep the game moving under pressure from a defender.

4. The introduction defenders forces the players to make more mistakes, so they must learn to make quick and correct decisions to avoid this.

5. The weight of the passes is key so their teammates can receive easily and then pass again.

6. Monitor the positioning of the players and their movement into space, making sure they provide the right angles to receive the next pass.

Coaching Points for the 3 Defenders

1. They should defend close together with small spaces in between them, making sure to use intelligent positioning.

2. The defenders start to learn and understand the right time to attack the ball and try to win it.

3. There needs to be an urgency to actively defend with at least one player trying to close down the ball carrier to force mistakes and win the ball for his team.

Positional 3 v 2 Dribbling Game with End Zones

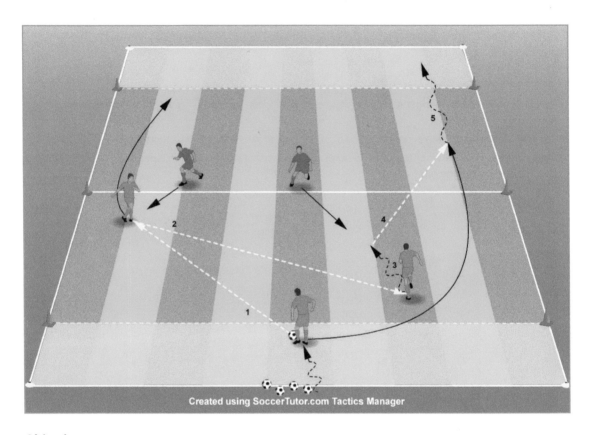

Created using SoccerTutor.com Tactics Manager

Objective

To develop passing, possession, player movement and collective defending.

Description

In a 12 x 20 yard area, we work with 5 players (3 orange attackers and 2 blue defenders) and position the cones as shown in the diagram so we have 2 end zones and a halfway line. The practice starts with an orange player from the end zone line. Both teams must start the practice from within their own half.

The orange players use teamwork to build up play and then score by dribbling the ball over the end zone line (1 point). The defenders work together to prevent this, win the ball and then try to score at the opposite end. The first team to score 3 points wins. When a goal is scored or the ball goes out of play, the practice starts again with the orange team from the end zone line.

Variation

You can add a neutral player ('Chameleon') who plays with the team in possession who can also score. Change the role of the 'Chameleon' every 5 minutes.

Coaching Points for Maintaining Posession

1. Be aware of your teammates free in space and keep the ball out of the reach of the defenders.

2. Dribble the ball into the free space, using simple changes in direction, and stopping/accelerating with the ball.

3. Players need to shield the ball, keeping their body in between the ball and the defender.

4. After playing the ball, players should then make movements to receive the ball back (maintain possession).

5. Keep yourself free of the defender so the ball can be played and you receive in space (keep moving).

6. Check away from the defender before moving to receive the ball.

Coaching Points for the 2 Defenders

1. Work together to maintain small distances between each other and block potential passing lanes.

2. Defend at an angle (using the correct body shape) to reduce the space and time for the player in possession.

3. The defenders start to learn and understand the right time to do attack the ball and try to win it.

4. There needs to be an urgency to actively defend with at least one player trying to close down the ball carrier to force mistakes and win the ball for his team.

Attack vs Defence 4 Goal Positional Game (3 v 2)

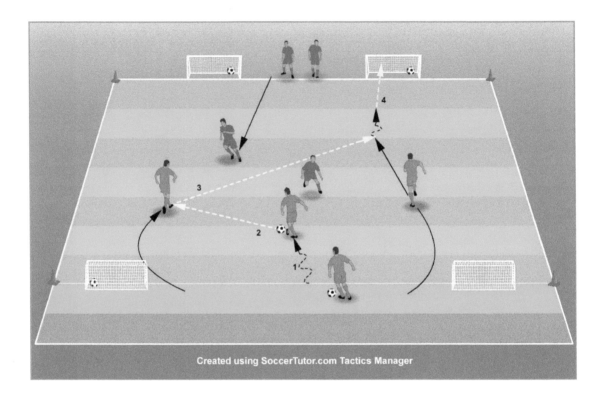

Created using SoccerTutor.com Tactics Manager

Description

In a 20 x 30 yard area, we have 8 players in total and play 3v2 with 4 goals. Both sets of players start from the ends of the pitch in between the 2 goals they are defending. The practice starts with an orange player who dribbles forwards.

The orange team's aim is to maintain possession of the ball, beat the defenders and then score in one of the mini goals. If the defenders win the ball, they then try to score in the mini goals at the opposite end.

If the ball goes out of play, the practice starts from the other end with the blues becoming the attackers with the same 3v2 advantage.

Variations

1. To make the practice harder for the attackers, move the 2 mini goals closer together, reduce the width of the area or create an offside line on the halfway line.

2. To make the practice harder for the defenders, move the 2 mini goals so they are further apart or increase the length of the area.

Coaching Points for the 3 Attackers

1. By moving the ball quickly and making intelligent movements, scoring opportunities can be created easily.

2. The weight of the passes is key so their teammates can receive easily and then pass or shoot.

3. The players learn how to keep the game moving under pressure from defenders.

4. Monitor the positioning of the players and their movement into space, making sure they provide the right angles to receive the next pass.

Coaching Points for the 2 Defenders

1. They should work well together with good communication, defending with small spaces in between them and making sure to use intelligent positioning.

2. The defenders start to learn and understand the right time to attack the ball and try to win it.

3. There needs to be an urgency to actively defend, with at least one player trying to close down the ball carrier to force mistakes and win the ball for his team.

Attack vs Defence Positional 2 Zone Game (3 v 2) with Goalkeepers

Created using SoccerTutor.com Tactics Manager

Description

In a 10 x 45 yard area, we have 8 players in total and play 3v2 with 2 goals and 2 goalkeepers. The practice starts with the orange goalkeeper who passes to a teammate and the 3v2 attack vs defence begins.

The orange team have 2 players at the back and 1 forward and their aim is to maintain possession of the ball, beat the defenders and then score in the goal past the goalkeeper.

If the defenders win the ball, they try to score at the opposite end (goal counts double). If the ball goes out of play, the practice starts from the other end with the blues becoming the attackers with the same 3v2 advantage.

Variations

1. To make the practice harder for the attackers, reduce the width of the area or create an offside line 15 yards from goal (as shown by the white dashed line in the diagram).

2. To make the practice harder for the defenders, increase the width of the area.

Coaching Points for the 3 Attackers

1. Lure in the defender in to exploit the free space in behind.

2. Play at a high pace to put pressure directly on the structure of the defending team.

3. The players need to demonstrate quick and intelligent decision making.

4. The players need to release the ball quickly after receiving, before being closed down by a defender.

5. There needs to be good positional play in this small area to create time/space for a through ball.

6. Short one-two passing combinations should be used.

7. Effective coordination and communication is needed between the 2 players at the back and the forward.

Building Up Play from the Goalkeeper in a Dynamic Practice

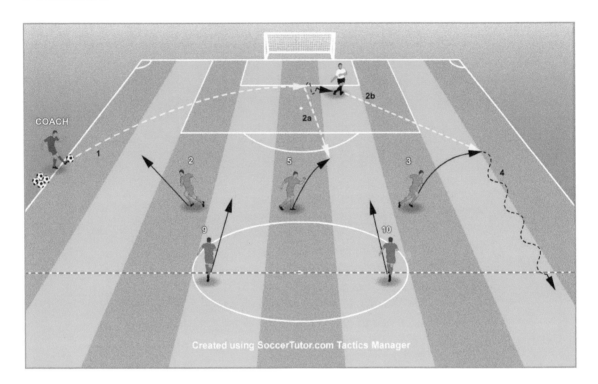

Objective

To improve positioning and to develop building up play from the back in a dynamic practice.

Description

Using half a pitch we have a goalkeeper, 3 defenders (orange) and 2 forwards (blue) who start in the positions shown in the diagram. The coach starts the practice from the sideline by passing the ball to the goalkeeper. As the ball is travelling to the goalkeeper, all 3 defenders make movements to receive the ball. The goalkeeper is aware of the oncoming forwards and must decide the right option. The aim of the defenders is to dribble the ball past the halfway line to score a goal. If the forwards win the ball, they try to score in the goal past the goalkeeper.

Coaching Points for the Goalkeeper

1. The goalkeeper should receive with the inside of the foot and play the ball quickly with the second touch.

2. The goalkeeper should choose which side to pass the ball based on the positioning of the blue forwards.

Coaching Points for the 3 Defenders

1. Two defenders should make themselves available to receive out wide.

2. The players should receive on the half turn and with their back foot, enabling them to then dribble forward.

3. The centre back provides an option in the middle and is also in a half turned position.

Dutch Academy Football Coaching (U10-11)

Formation Specific 5 v 4 Small Sided Game (1-2-1 vs 2-1)

Created using SoccerTutor.com Tactics Manager

Objective

To improve positioning and to develop building up play, finishing and collective defending in a competitive small sided game.

Description

In a 35 x 40 yard area, we play a 5v4 small sided game. The orange attacking team are in a 1-2-1 formation and the blue defending team are in a 2-1 formation.

The practice starts with the orange goalkeeper and the orange team build up play and try to score in the big goal. If the blue team win the ball, they then try to score in the goal at the opposite end.

If a goal is scored or the ball goes out of play, 1 orange player leaves the field and the extra blue player enters. We then start again with the blue goalkeeper and the blue team have the same aims with their 5v4 numerical advantage. After a predetermined period of time, change the formations of the teams around.

Variations

1. To make the practice harder for the attackers, reduce the width of the area, reward the defending team if they score a goal by making it count double or create an offside line 10 yards from goal.

2. To make the practice harder for the defenders, increase the length of the area.

Coaching Points for the Attacking Team

1. The attacking players should try to score as quickly as possible. If a player is in space, he should take the opportunity to shoot at goal.

2. There needs to be good movement with and without the ball to create space and scoring opportunities.

3. The players should be aware of their teammate and pass to them if they are in a better position. This practice starts to develop 'playmaking'.

4. If the goalkeeper collects/saves the ball, he should then pass quickly to continue the game.

5. Encourage the players to use feints/moves to beat they have learnt to unbalance the defender and quickly move the ball in the opposite direction.

Coaching Points for the Defending Team

1. The positional play is very important, so the defenders learn to defend their goal and prevent passes in behind.

2. When applying pressure, it is important to force the ball carrier to one side (side-on body shape).

3. Timing the right moment to move forward to try to steal the ball is key.

4. Try to prevent shots on goal and get in position to block shots.

5. Do not retreat towards your own goal.

6. Communicate with the goalkeeper and work together to defend.

7. Follow up shots to collect or clear the ball if the goalkeeper is unable to hold onto the ball.

Formation Specific Dynamic 4 v 3 Small Sided Game with 4 Goals (1-2-1 vs 2-1)

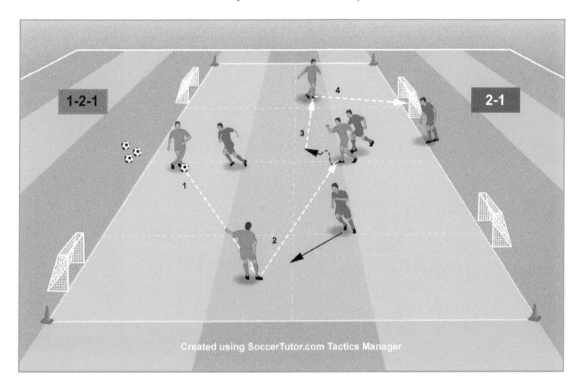

Objective

To improve positioning, develop build up play, finishing and collective defending in a competitive game.

Description

In a 20 x 40 yard area, we play a 4v3 small sided game with 4 mini goals in the positions shown. The orange attacking team are in a 1-2-1 formation and the blue defending team are in a 2-1 formation.

The practice starts with the deepest orange player either in the middle or in the corner. The orange team build up play and try to score in the mini goals, which are 7 yards away from the sideline. The blue team defend collectively, try to win the ball and then try to score in the mini goals (3 yards from sideline) at the opposite end.

If a goal is scored or the ball goes out of play, 1 orange player leaves the field and the extra blue player enters. We then start again with the blue team in possession and they have the same aims with a 4v3 numerical advantage.

Variations

1. To make the practice harder for the attackers, reduce the width of the area or move the goals closer together.
2. To make the practice harder for the defenders, increase the length of the area.

Formation Specific 4 v 3 Play and Dribbling in a Small Sided Game with End Zones (1-2-1 vs 1-2)

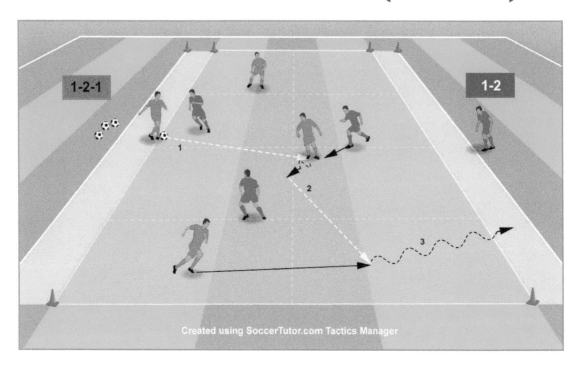

Objective

To improve positioning, develop build up play, finishing and collective defending in a competitive game.

Description

In a 20 x 40 yard area, we mark out 2 end zones (3-5 yards in length) and play a 4v3 game.

The practice starts with an orange player from the end zone line. The orange team are in a 1-2-1 formation and the blue team are in a 1-2 formation.

The orange players use teamwork to build up play and then score by dribbling the ball over the end zone line (1 point). The defenders work together to prevent this, win the ball and then try to score at the opposite end.

The first team to score 3 points wins. When a goal is scored or the ball goes out of play, the practice starts again with the orange team from the end zone line.

After every goal that is scored, 1 blue player rotates with the outside player so they get rest. After a predetermined period of time, change the roles of the teams.

Variations

1. To make the practice harder for the attackers, reduce the width of the area or add cone gates on the end zone line that the players have to dribble through to score.

2. To make the practice harder for the defenders, increase the length of the area.

Coaching Points for the Attacking Team

1. The focus of this practice is building up play (playmaking), attacking the free space and dribbling over the goal line.

2. Dribble the ball into the free space, using simple changes in direction and stopping/accelerating with the ball.

3. The speed of play should be high with the players acting quickly.

4. Good decision making is needed to judge the game situation and choose the right timing and direction of passes.

5. Players need to shield the ball, keeping their body in between the ball and the defender.

Coaching Points for the Defending Team

1. Work together to maintain small distances between each other and block potential passing lanes.

2. The key to this practice is positional defending, keeping compact and having good communication to move as a unit to deny space in behind.

3. The defenders start to learn and understand the right time to do attack the ball and try to win it.

4. The players should constantly be aware of the position of the ball and if one player moves to close down the ball carrier, another defender must provide cover behind.

CHAPTER 9

FORMATION SPECIFIC SMALL SIDED GAMES

Small Sided Games

Instructions for Attacking in Small Sided Games

- Make the space as large as possible and play from your position.

- Do not move into the same area that a teammate/opponent is already occupying. Choose a position that you can most easily receive the ball and do not go behind a defender where there is no path to pass to you.

- Check away from your marker before moving to receive in space.

- Do not all move towards the ball.

- Do not all move away from the ball.

- It is important to have 2 passing options at all times.

- There should often be an option behind the ball so that possession can be maintained.

- Use a high speed of play with an action immediately following the last action, and continue to do it.

- Have a player available out wide, using the full width of the space available.

- The player in the forward position should be close enough to goal so he is able to shoot quickly after receiving.

Instructions for Defending in Small Sided Games

- Be aware of the position of the ball and your opponents at all times.

- Defend close together (with small spaces in between the players).

- Force the play out wide and away from the goal (use the correct body shape when pressing).

- Give each other good cover, making sure to work well together.

- Always choose to defend the most dangerous situation which could lead to a shot on goal i.e. always look to get between the ball and the goal (goal side position).

- Do not go to ground too quickly, making sure to stay on your feet as long as possible (do not over commit).

- Ensure that the opponent with the ball can not play a pass in behind.

- Players need to use their own initiative and actions to keep pressure on the attackers (keep them busy and force quick decisions).

- Face your opponent head on as much as possible and do not turn your back on him.

- Judge the right time to commit and win the ball from an opponent e.g. when they take a heavy touch.

- Recognise a weak pass from your opponent and try to intercept the ball.

- When the opposition use a one-two combination, make sure to follow the player's run and not the ball.

Formation Specific 5 v 5 Small Sided Game with 4 Goals (4-1 vs 2-3)

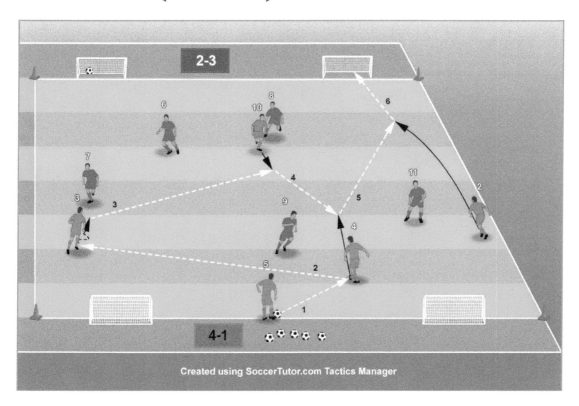

Created using SoccerTutor.com Tactics Manager

Objective

To improve positioning and to develop building up play, finishing and collective defending in a competitive small sided game.

Description

In a 30 x 40 yard area, we play a normal 5v5 small sided game with 4 mini goals in the positions shown. The orange team are in a 4-1 formation and the blue team are in a 2-3 formation.

The players play in specific positions and practice building up play, finishing on goal and collectively defending as a team. Monitor whether your teaching has been understood and whether the objective has been achieved.

Refer to the coaching points at the beginning and end of this chapter.

Formation Specific 6 v 6 Small Sided Game (4-1 vs 2-3)

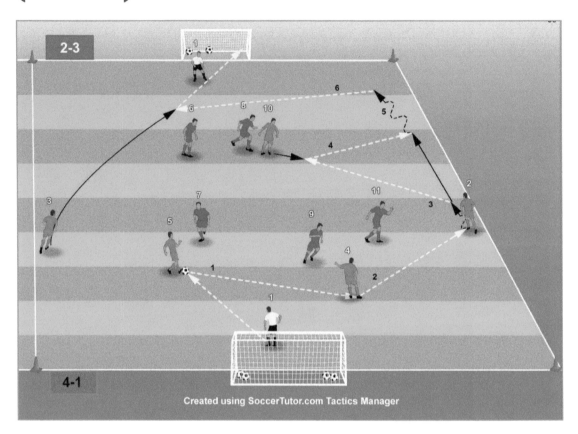

Created using SoccerTutor.com Tactics Manager

Objective

To improve positioning and to develop building up play, finishing and collective defending in a competitive small sided game.

Description

In a 40 x 50 yard area, we play a normal 6v6 small sided game with 2 large goals. The orange team are in a 4-1 formation and the blue team are in a 2-3 formation.

The players play in specific positions and practice building up play, finishing on goal and collectively defending as a team. Monitor whether your teaching has been understood and whether the objective has been achieved.

Refer to the coaching points at the beginning and end of this chapter.

Formation Specific 7 v 7 Small Sided Game (4-2 vs 3-3)

Objective

To improve positioning and to develop building up play, finishing and collective defending in a competitive small sided game.

Description

In a 50 x 60 yard area, we play a normal 7v7 small sided game with 2 large goals. The orange team are in a 4-2 formation and the blue team are in a 3-3 formation.

The players play in specific positions and practice building up play, finishing on goal and collectively defending as a team. Monitor whether your teaching has been understood and whether the objective has been achieved.

Refer to the coaching points at the beginning and end of this chapter.

Formation Specific 8 v 8 Small Sided Game (4-2-1 vs 1-3-3)

Objective

To improve positioning and to develop building up play, finishing and collective defending in a competitive small sided game.

Description

In a 55 x 65 yard area, we play a normal 8v8 small sided game with 2 large goals. The orange team are in a 4-2-1 formation and the blue team are in a 1-3-3 formation.

The players play in specific positions and practice building up play, finishing on goal and collectively defending as a team. Monitor whether your teaching has been understood and whether the objective has been achieved.

Refer to the coaching points at the beginning and end of this chapter.

Formation Specific 9 v 9 Small Sided Game (3-2-3 vs 3-2-3)

Objective

To improve positioning and to develop building up play, finishing and collective defending in a competitive small sided game.

Description

In a 60 x 65 yard area, we play a normal 9v9 small sided game with 2 large goals. The orange team are in a 3-2-3 formation and the blue team are also in a 3-2-3 formation.

The players play in specific positions and practice building up play, finishing on goal and collectively defending as a team. Monitor whether your teaching has been understood and whether the objective has been achieved.

Refer to the coaching points at the beginning and end of this chapter.

Coaching Points for Attacking in Formation Specific Small Sided Games

1. Build up play as a team, but always look to create opportunities to score goals.

2. Use the full width and length of the area with good positioning and movement to stretch the defending team.

3. Intelligent and quick decisions are needed.

4. Whenever possible, try to play the ball forward and in behind the defence.

5. With a player positioned out wide, you create the option for a longer pass to switch the play.

6. Try to find the optimum position on the pitch to make sure you are in space and can receive.

7. Maintaining possession is the foundation to building up play.

8. Players should receive the ball half-turned to speed up the transition to the next pass, dribble or shot on goal.

Coaching Points for Defending in Formation Specific Small Sided Games

1. Work together as a collective unit to prevent shots on goals and win the ball.

2. Shield the goal with good body positioning (goal side position).

3. Always play close to each other (compact).

4. Apply pressure on the opponent in possession.

5. Provide sharp cover in the vicinity of the ball.

6. If the ball is given away, make sure to provide very quick cover by tracking back into dangerous areas.

7. Do not make fouls.

8. Avoid putting pressure directly on the player with the ball if you anticipate a potential long pass.

9. After winning the ball, see if you can score directly or you can create a chance by playing the ball forward or in behind.

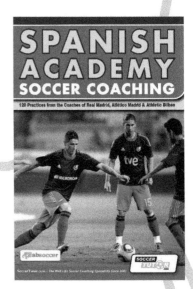

Printed in the USA
CPSIA information can be obtained
at www.ICGtesting.com
LVHW060824250124
769490LV00087B/3605